THE CAUSES, EVILS, AND CURES, OF HEART AND CHURCH DIVISIONS

EXTRACTED FROM THE WORKS OF BURROUGHS AND BAXTER.

Francis Asbury
One of the Bishops of the Methodist Episcopal Church.

Introduction by
John N. Oswalt

Seek peace and *pursue* it. —Psalm xxxiv. 14.

SCHMUL
PUBLISHING

This Schmul Publishing Co. edition is not a scanned facsimile of a used book. It has not been "updated" or edited into modern English, punctuation or grammar, but is accurate to the author's own style and usage. The text has been carefully proofread for accuracy and formatted for easier reading by today's readers. Every effort has been made to prevent disordered text. The only intentional alteration is the standardization of chapter numbers for the modern reader's ease of use.

Second Edition
Published by Schmul Publishing Co.
PO Box 776
Nicholasville, KY 40340

ISBN 10: 0-88019-650-5
ISBN 13: 978-0-88019-650-5

Visit us on the Internet at www.wesleyanbooks.com, or order direct from the publisher by calling 800-772-6657, or by writing to the above address.

Contents

2

Considerations/93

3

Directions/105

Introduction

IT IS A PLEASURE to introduce this new edition of Bishop Francis Asbury's only book, a book that is, in fact, a compilation of two other books that the father of American Methodism found particularly appropriate and helpful to his situation. That situation was church division, a subject that is much on the minds of American Methodists today. Although the situation today is different from the ones that Asbury faced, many of the issues discussed continue to be relevant.

The authors, and Asbury, by extension, are concerned to identify the personal issues that have often led to division. One cannot read very much in the letters of Paul without confronting these matters. How often the Apostle addresses pride, envy, jealousy, self-serving, and personal opinions as underlying causes of division, and in this book these matters are dealt with in detail. When divisions arise from these causes, they are always to be condemned. This book can be recommended precisely because it will help the reader to identify in himself or herself, most of all, these tendencies and to allow the Holy Spirit to deal with them.

All this being said, it must be pointed out that the fracturing that is presently occurring in the United Methodist denomination is not, by and large, the result of these causes. To be sure, there may be isolated instances where these are in play, and if they are, that ought to be faced and dealt with, but they are not the central issue. Some might say differences of opinion over human sexuality are the causes of the divisions, but that issue is only the presenting cause. The real cause is much deeper. It is one that has been entrenching itself in the denomination for a century in deeper and deeper ways. The impact of this matter was often muted throughout the intervening years and its significance, while pointed out by some lone voices,[1] could be overlooked by the many. Now its effect has become unmistakably clear.

What is this issue? It is the issue of biblical authority. For a century and more Methodist seminaries have been chipping away at this bedrock foundation of the Christian faith. If the Bible is not the divinely authorized revelation of God as to the meaning of life, the nature of the human problem, and the provision of God for the solution of the problem, the Christian religion is a tissue of lies, a whistling in the dark as we pass the graveyard. The Bible's divine authority is irreplaceably important. If it is only the product of naïve persons attempting to find a way around the grim realities of life, then it is not to be piously paraded but to be discarded.

Yet, the work of biblical scholarship has been precisely to erode any trace of a divine hand in the book and its claims. So, we began by denying Mosaic authorship of the Pentateuch, and then the historicity of the Exodus, and then the reality of the Conquest, and then the king-

---

[1] In the 1920s Henry Clay Morrison, then president of Asbury College (now University) brought into existence a theological school that would espouse orthodox Methodist doctrine while maintaining a separate existence from the denomination whose official seminaries were already being seduced away from the truth.

doms of David and Solomon. This was accompanied by the denial of the Virgin Birth and the consequent Deity of Christ and the Bodily Resurrection of Christ. But we were lulled to sleep by the fact that while more and more pastors, having been misled by their seminary professors, were espousing these ideas, the denomination did not consider changing its official stance upon biblical authority and the doctrinal positions emerging from that authority (except, perhaps, in a few smoke-filled rooms).

It was only when there came about a movement in the mid-1970s to change the denomination's official statements on sexuality that it became increasingly clear what had happened to us. The Bible's endorsement of life-long marriage between a man and a woman and its condemnation of any form of sexual expression outside of such a marriage relationship is unmistakable.

It is appropriate here to say a word about this matter in relation to biblical authority. It is sometimes said that, in fact, positions relating to sexuality are really matters of opinion and not of biblical authority since there are biblical pronouncements and positions to which Christians no longer adhere, such as commands to offer sacrifices and the acceptance of slavery as a fact of life. This is a worthy argument, and one that ought not to be dismissed. At the same time, it is rather easily addressed. Not all the mandates of the Old Testament are to be considered absolute. Some, such as sacrifice, are specifically removed by the New Testament; others, such as circumcision and sabbath-keeping, are made optional. But others, such as adultery and homosexual practice continue to be prohibited. There is the principle: when the New Testament confirms what the Old Testament requires, it is incumbent upon the Christian to obey.

The matter of slavery is different. First, and of vital importance, nowhere does the Bible, Old or New Testament, *command* a Christian to keep slaves. It was only permitted in a world where slavery was the unquestioned norm. Why was it not condemned? It was not condemned for the same reason that civil obedience was commanded; Christ and his followers were not interested in fomenting a social revolution. What they taught about humanity in relation to God would necessarily revolutionize society, but from the direction of individual to society, not the reverse. Thus, we may say today, with thanks, that biblical principles lead inevitably to the conclusion that no person should enslave another.

But what attitudes shall we display as we withdraw from a denomination that has become apostate? Asbury's book will tell us that we should do so with love for those from whom we depart. We should do so with sorrow and regret. There should not be a shred of triumphalism or self-righteous pride. Let us offer sincere prayer for the conversion of those who have abandoned biblical authority. Let us avoid any sort of finger-pointing or any judgmental attitudes. Let us pay attention to ourselves and should there be recriminations levelled against us, let us receive them with quietness and humility and no breath of bitter self-defense. Let us behave in a manner that will confirm the truth of the gospel (1 Cor 9:23).

—JOHN N. OSWALT
January 4, 2023

Advertisement.

OUR DISCIPLINE RECOMMENDS (PART i, ch. iv, §16) "a serious perusal of the 'Causes, Evils, and Cures of Heart and Church Divisions.'" The work has long been out of print, so that the recommendation could not be complied with. A new edition is now furnished at a low price, with a view to its general circulation. Recent events have tended, perhaps, to weaken the spirit of union among us— it may be well for us to scrutinize our hearts and lives more closely. "If we are united, what can stand before us? If we divide, we shall destroy ourselves, the work of God, and the souls of our people."

—J. M'CLINTOCK.

January 1, 1849.

To the Ministers and Members of the Methodist Episcopal Church.

DEAR BRETHREN, — IN THE course of my reading, some years ago, I met with an old book, written by a worthy pastor in the church, Mr. Jeremiah Burroughs, on *Heart Divisions, the Evil of our Times*. Feeling at that time the pain of a partial separation in spirit and practice from some who were as my brethren and sons in the gospel, that book proved as a balm and a blessing to my soul. I saw so clearly the evil consequences of a division, and how good and pleasant a thing it is for brethren to dwell together in unity, that I began to abridge my obsolete, but valuable book, and earnestly wished, prayed, and strove, for unanimity.

Soon after, I met with another old book, entitled *The Cure of Church Divisions*; written by that venerable servant of God, the John Wesley of his day, in wisdom, affection, zeal, and a pacific spirit; I mean Mr. Richard Baxter, of precious memory. Being highly pleased with his evangelical sentiments, I concluded to make an extract from both, not doubting but it might be of great service to the church of Christ.

And now I recommend it to all ministers of the gospel, and professing Christians of every denomination, into whose hands it may come, beseeching them to read it carefully, and with much prayer, that they may cultivate a spirit of unity and brotherly love.

I remain, dear brethren, your servant for Christ's sake,

—FRANCIS ASBURY.

Part I
The Causes of Divisions.

1.
Distempers that Divide.

Pride the Chief Dividing Distemper.

PRIDE IS THE GREATEST master of misrule in the world; it is the great incendiary in the soul of man, in families, in towns, in cities, in all societies, in church and state: this wind causeth tempests to arise. Prov. xiii, 10: "Only by pride cometh contention." The Holy Ghost singles out PRIDE, as the only cause of all contentions, because it is the chief; though there be many in a riot, the whole is usually laid upon the ring-leaders. Pride is the ringleader to all riots, divisions, disturbances among us. Prov. xxi, 24: "Proud and haughty scorner is his name, who dealeth in proud wrath." Pride may be well indicated for the great common barrator, or wrangler, in all our towns and cities; it makes woful troubles wherever it comes.

We read in Scripture of the manna that God gave his people; such was the nature of it, that the heat of the sun melted it. You will say, "How would it then endure the heat of the oven? for they baked it in the oven." Yet, so it was of a strange kind of nature, that it could bear the heat of the oven, and not the heat of the sun. Even of such a temper are our hearts; the heat of the sun of prosperity dissolves us, causes us to run one from another: but the heat of the fire of affliction bakes us, brings us and settles us together; it makes us to be one, it takes away our rawness, it consumes many of our ill humours, and so composes our spirits into one. The stupidness of our hearts is such, that we do not make our brethren's case our own; but we for the present having some more liberty than formerly, are lifted up, and in the pride of our hearts push at our brethren, and smite our fellow servants: if the troubles be at a little distance from us, though we even hear the cries of our brethren who are in the midst of them, yet we foolishly bless ourselves in our present ease, enjoyments, and hopes, as if our flesh must be spared, our estates and enjoyments continued, yea, raised, whatever becomes of others. O sinful vain spirits, befooled and hardened by their pride!

But what are the several workings of pride that make such a stir in the world?

Answ. A proud man thinks himself too great to be crossed. Shall I bear this? I will make you know what it is to do such things against me! He thinks it a great dishonour to himself to bear anything; therefore he must needs quarrel and contend, if it is but to show what a man of spirit he is, or to show that he is a man of such worth, that whatever others bear, it is not fit for him to bear it. It is but reason that such a man as he should make men, who will presume to cross him, to yield to him, to stoop under him. Now when one proud man thinks it a dishonour to him to put up with wrongs from another, who it may be is as proud as himself, and he thinks it a dishonour for him to put up with wrongs, what peace can there be? Some wrongs must be put up with, but proud men will never agree who shall begin.

PRIDE makes men swell beyond their bounds: the way to keep all things in union is for every man to keep within his bounds: the swelling beyond tends to the breaking all in pieces. Hab. ii, 5: "He is a proud man, neither keepeth at home, who enlargeth his desire as hell, and cannot be satisfied." If any humour of the body goeth beyond its bounds, it brings much trouble to it; the health and peace of the body consist in the keeping of every humour within its vessel, and due proportion.

PRIDE hardens men's hearts. Dan. v, 10: "His mind is hardened in his pride." If you would have things cleave, you must have them soft; two flints will not join: the Spaniard hath a proverb, lime and stone will make a wall; if one be hard, yet if the other be yielding, there may be joining, and good may be done, not else.

PRIDE causes men to despise the persons, actions, and sufferings, of others; and nothing is more insufferable to a man's spirit than to be vilified. A proud man despises what others do, and others what he does; every man, next to his person, desires the honour of his actions; if these two be contemned, his sufferings will like-wise be contemned by the proud: this also goes very near to a man; one man thinks what another man suffers is nothing, no matter what becomes of him; another thinks his sufferings nothing, and no matter what becomes of him. O at what a distance now are men's hearts one from another!

PRIDE causes every man to desire to be taken notice of, to have an eminency in some thing or another; if he cannot be eminent on one side, he will get to the other; he must be taken notice of, one way or other; when he is in a good and peaceable way, God makes some use of him; yet because he is not observed and looked upon as eminent, he will rather turn to some other way, to contend, strive, to oppose, or anything, that he may be taken notice of, to be somebody, that he may not go out of the world without some noise. "What, shall such a man as I, of such parts, such approved abilities, so endued by God to do some eminent service, be laid aside, and nobody regard me? I must set upon some notable work, something that may draw the eye of observance upon me!" I have read of a young man who set Diana's temple on fire, and being asked the reason, he said, "That he might have a name, that the people might talk of him." Because he could not be famous for doing good, he would for doing evil. Proud spirits will venture the setting the temple of God, yea, church and state, on fire, that they may have a name; whatever they do or suffer to get a name, they will rather venture, than die in obscurity; *that* above all things they cannot bear.

A proud man makes his will the rule of his actions, and would have it be the rule of other men's too; and other men being proud, would have their wills the rule of their actions, and of his too. Thus the blustering wind of PRIDE in men's hearts causes them to jostle one against another, and so to split themselves one upon another; as where many ships lie together, a violent wind breaking their anchor-cables, causes them to dash one upon another, and so to make shipwreck even in the haven.

Proud men will venture upon things unseemly; thinking their esteem and greatness will bear them out; and others who are proud, will venture upon the like, upon the same ground, for every man is ready to high thoughts of himself. Psa. xix, 14: "Deliver me from presumptuous sins," a *superbis*, so some, *ab insolentibus* so others, from proud, from insolent sins.

If there is anything to be done that is conceived to be mean and low, a proud man will strive to put it upon others, and others who are proud, will strive to put it upon him; and if it be a work of credit, then he seeks it to himself, and others seek it to themselves, and hence are jarrings and divisions.

One proud man thinks himself the only worthy man

to have his counsel followed, and his desires satisfied; and the other thinks himself the man that should have his counsel followed, and his desires satisfied: and thus men struggle and oppose one another.

Here we see what a make-bate PRIDE is; that which Tertullus said to Felix (Acts xxiv, 2) is true of humility: "By thee we enjoy great quietness;" but the contrary is as true of pride: "By thee are made woful divisions, by thee we suffer miserable disturbances." Though there be no occasion of quarrel, yet pride will make some; only by pride comes contention, as before. Prov. xiii, 10.

Now let every man look into his own heart, and see what pride hath been, and still is there, and be humbled before the Lord for this. All you contentious, froward, quarrelsome people, you are charged this day from God with being men and women of proud spirits, and what evil there is in our sad divisions, that pride in your bosom is a great cause of it. St. Paul "did keep under his body, lest after he had preached to others, he should become a castaway," or a reprobate. Let us all look to it, and especially ministers, lest after all our profession and glorious shows, we at last become reprobates, at least such as God may cast out for destruction, even in this world, taking no delight in making use of; what, in such times as these to have hearts swoln and lifted up with" pride? God is now about staying the pride of the earth. How unseasonable and dangerous for a mariner to have his topsails up, and all spread in a violent storm; it is time then to pull down all, lest he sink irrecoverably. The point of a needle will let the wind out of a bladder, and shall not the swords of God, the swords of war, and plague, that have got so deep into our bowels, let out the windy pride of our hearts? "The haughtiness of men shall be bowed down, and the Lord himself will be exalted." The Lord humbleth us, that he may reconcile us, not only to himself, but to one another.

Self-Love is Another Dividing Distemper.

Phil. ii, 3: "Let nothing be done through strife." Verse 4: "Look not every man on his own things, but every man also on the things of others." This is the cause of strife, because men look so much on their own things. Many will have no peace, except their own party be followed; Jehu like, "what hast thou to do with peace? follow me." It is not peace, but party, that they mind. *Maxima pars studiorum est studium partium*; that is, the greatest part of their studies is to study sides and parties. Luther upon Psa. cxxvii hath a notable speech: "I am of that opinion" says he, "that monarchies would continue longer than they do, were it not for that same little *pronoun (Ego)* that same *(I)* myself." Yea, certainly, could this same SELF be laid aside, all governments and societies would not only continue longer, but flourish better. "Self-love is the cause of our divisions;" where this prevails, men love to take in all to themselves.

Those who are actuated by self-love, have no common ends to join them, therefore they cannot close; if they be employed in public service, they quickly work to their private ends. Thus many at the first: O who but they for the public, for the common good! But there being a principle of self within, and some difficulty rising, they warped to their own ends, and divided from those they were employed with. Men's private ends are narrow, they cannot drive on them, but they will meet with one another, and jostle one another, quarrel, contend, and fight for the way, as cartmen do when they meet in narrow streets, and boatmen in narrow passages. If we had public ends, our way would be broad enough, we might go on peaceably and comfortably, without prejudice against one another. If a man lived alone, then he might go on quietly in his own way, only God would meet him in it; but seeing men live in the world among others, they must consider, that if they will drive on their own designs, and work their own ends, other men have designs and ends to drive on and work as well as they: it is therefore impossible but you will cross and be crossed; you will vex and fret at others, and others will vex and fret at you.

When anything doth but smell of SELF, it begins to be loathed; let a man have never such excellent parts, do never such excellent things, yet if SELF appears, the loveliness and glory of all is gone; therefore those men that act SELF, had need be very cunning to keep in and hide it; herein appears what a vile thing SELF is, that though in truth it acts all, and receives the incomes of all, yet it dares not appear, but lies skulking under all the covers it can. How vile is this SELF for which all must be done, which thou makest thy God, yet cannot in the least appear, but is odious and abominable to every one! Yea, it is conscious to itself that it is so, and therefore dares not appear; yet the acting of it is very mischievous to all human societies.

There is this wickedness in SELF-LOVE, that even those things that men acknowledge to be right and good in the general, yet if they shall not particularly suit with, something they would have, it will put men upon the opposing; and what peace and union can there be among men, if what they will grant, and commend to be good, yet when it falls across to them, they will oppose, and contend against?

SELF causes men not to see their own evils, or if they do, to indulge themselves in them; but to be quick-sighted and severe in the discovering and opposing those evils that are in others, and this causes many breaches and fallings out. We may apply that of the apostle, 1 Cor. xiii, "Love covereth a multitude of faults," to self-love. Selfish men see but little evil in themselves— all is ever well with them, whatever others do; and the more they indulge themselves, the more severe they are to others; but Christ would have the quite contrary, severity to ourselves, but indulgence to others; those that are so, are the most peaceable men. Matt. xviii, 8: "If thy hand or foot offend thee, pluck them off, and cast them from thee; or if thine eye offend thee, pluck it out and cast it from thee." We must deal severely with ourselves in those things that are as near and as dear to us as our hands and eyes; but verse 15, when Christ gives orders how we are to deal with our brethren, he then requires more moderation: "If thy brother offend thee, go and tell him his fault between thee and him alone;" if he will not hear thee, then take with thee one or two more, and see what thou canst do with him in that way; yea, and after that, tell the church; not presently cut him off, and cast him away, as you must do when your hand or eye offends you. If men have any indulgence, let it be toward their brethren; if they have any severity, let them exercise that toward themselves. Pliny says of himself: "That he so passed by other men's offences, as if himself were the greatest offender, and he was so severe against himself, as if he meant to pardon none." If it were so with us, we should live at more peace one with another than we do.

These were wont to be entire friends; how came they to break off? what unkindness hath befallen them? None at all, only that principle of SELF was not so fully fed as it would be; upon that they began to be reserved, and so strange, and at last quite fell off from one another, from former love and friendship, and then every little thing caused grudgings between them.

SELF sets men's wits on work, in all cunning craftiness, to fetch others about to their own ends, and this goes as much against a man's spirit as anything; when he comes to discern it, no man can bear to be circumvented, to be made serviceable only to another man's ends. The more cunning there is in it, the more odious and abominable it is to a man's spirit; when it comes once to be discerned, a man cannot bear it. Crooked windings are the goings of the serpent: but if a man shall not only seek to make use of another to serve his own turn by him, but after he hath done that, then to cast him off to shift for himself; this is so provoking a thing, that it makes breaches irreconcilable.

When one is for SELF, in his ways, he makes another to be so in his; as a man, by conversing with the froward, learns to be froward; so many, who have heretofore had plain hearts, full of love and sweetness, yet, by being acquainted much with selfish political men, learn to be so too. I see how he looks to himself in everything, fetches about this way and that way, but still it terminates in self at last; I perceived it not at my first acquaintance with him, and then my heart was let out to him fully; but now I see every man is for himself, and why should not I be so too? And what then is like to become of the public?

Surely this selfishness is very vile in the eyes of God. God hath made us members of a community; the universe is maintained by union, therefore the creatures will venture the destroying themselves in going contrary to their natures, rather than there should not be union in the world; that which they do in a natural way, we should do by the strength of reason, much more by grace.

O foolish heart, that in such a time as this art selfish, when the danger is public! as in a storm, when the ship is in danger, if every mariner should be busy about his own cabin, dressing and painting that, what infinite sottish folly were it? and is it not our case! It were just with God to leave thee to thyself hereafter, if thou wilt look so much to thyself now. Ezek. xxii, 16: "And thou shalt take thine inheritance in thyself, in the sight of the heathen, and thou shalt know that I am the Lord." This is in a way of threat, as appears, if you compare it with ver. 14, 15. Wo to us if God leaves us to ourselves. I have heard of a fool being left in a chamber, and the door locked, and all the people gone, he cries out of the window, "O myself, myself! O myself!" nothing came from him but "O myself." Such fools have we among us now; nothing but self is in their thoughts, their hearts, and endeavours. The apostle's complaint (Phil. ii, 21) may justly be ours: "All seek their own, not the things which are Jesus Christ's:" their own things; that is, says Chrysostom, their pleasure, and their security, their temporal commodities, their profits, and their honors: so others: why are not the comforts, the safeties, the honours of the saints, the things of Christ? doth not Christ own them? are they not under his protection and care?

Answ. Yes, and he would own them more, if we owned them less; the more we deny them, the more hath he a care of them: we may, by our giving them up to the honour of Christ, make them to be among the number of his things, and then they would be precious indeed; but by desiring them, using them, rejoicing in them, in reference to ourselves, Christ accounts them not among his things; things of a higher nature are his things; the glory of his Father, the propagation of the gospel, the spiritual good of his people, and the things of eternal life, they are his things; let us make his things ours, and he will make our things his.

Envy a Dividing Distemper.

ENVY is a squint-eyed fool. Job v, 2: "Envy slayeth the silly one." James iii, 14: "If ye have bitter envying and strife in your hearts." Envy is a bitter thing, and causes strife, and makes that bitter too: so verse 16: "Where envying and strife is." Gal. v, 20: "Hatred, variance, emulations, wrath, strife, seditions, heresies, envyings." 1 Cor. iii, 3: "There is among you envying, strife, and divisions." ENVY made divisions between angels and men; it was the first sin, not the first-born of the devil, but that which turned angels into devils. The first heart division among men was between Cain and Abel, and what caused it but ENVY? who can stand before envy? she is subtle, undermining, dares not appear at the first; but if she cannot be satisfied with her underworks, then she flings, rends, frets, and fights, uses violence, seeks to raise a contrary faction, falls on anything in the world so mischief may be done, let what will become of God's glory, of service to the public, of saving souls: rather than that esteem, respect, and honour, that otherwise might be had, should not be obtained, all must come under, all must be serviceable to this base lust: rather than the glory of an envious man must be eclipsed, God himself and his earth must be darkened. O hideous wickedness, and high impudence against the God of heaven! ENVY divides in counsels, in instruments, actions, and in all proceedings; she will make use of good to oppose that which is good; if she cannot raise evil men to oppose good, she will seek to get good men to oppose; she would make God contrary to himself, she would strike at God with his own sword. Phil. i, 14: "Some preach Christ out of envy." As ENVY makes use of good for evil, so God makes use of this evil for good. Many seek to excel in preaching, or otherwise, by this means, and says St. Paul: "Howsoever I do rejoice, and will rejoice." When you see a man seeking to rake and gather together all he can of any mistakes, distempers, disorders, miscarriages, by hearsays, letters, or any way, so that by it he may fill up his dung-cart; and for the good, the grace or gifts of God in men, those are laid aside, or passed slightingly over; if at all mentioned, it is with some dirt mingled; surely this is an envious man, fitted for strife and debate, whom God permits to be an affliction to his people in raising up a spirit of strife and contention, and causing divisions among them; like the kite, who passes over fair meadows and pleasant fields, not regarding them, till she meets with a carrion, and then falls and fastens; now she is upon her prey where she would be; how pleasant is it to some men to hear of, or find out, evils in others whom they do not love? To say no worse, you know it hath been an old practice to seek to get anything by reports, or any other way that might blast the professors of religion; and how glad were they! how did it please them at the heart, if they could meet with anything that might serve their turn!

The Holy Ghost says, that *envy is rottenness to the bones*; this is applied, by a learned man, to such as are chief in church and commonwealth, who are, as it were, the bones, the strength, the support, of the societies where they are; ENVY, says he, is often found among them, and it is rottenness to them. This vile sin has caused a rot in many men of eminent abilities and places, who might otherwise have done much service for God and his people in church and state. O it is a mischievous sin! "Take away envy," says Augustine, "and what you have is mine; take away envy, and what I have is yours." We read, Acts xi, of Barnabas, that he was a good man, and full of the Holy Ghost, and he was a man of a cleaving disposition, of a uniting temper: verse 23, "He exhorteth them that with full purpose of heart they would cleave unto the Lord." This man was free from envy: for the text says, "When he had seen the grace of God he was glad;" he rejoiced in, and blessed God for the grace he saw in his saints. " Do you envy for my sake?" says Moses; "I would to God all the people of the Lord did prophesy." Moses was a fit man for public service, who was so void of ENVY; no men are so fit for public service as those who can bless God that he is pleased to make use of others as well as them, yea beyond themselves. It was a good spirit of that gracious, holy, old disciple, Mr. Dod, "I would to God," said he, "I were the worst minister in England;" not wishing himself worse than he was, but all ministers better.

Passion is a Dividing Distemper.

Those men who, upon every trifle, are all on fire by their PASSIONS, and what in them lies, set others on fire, do exceedingly disturb the peace of those places where they live, and those societies of which they are members: their hot passions cause the climate where they live to be like the torrid zone, too hot for any to live near them. Christ is the Prince of peace, and the devil is the prince of division: hence that expression of the Holy Ghost, Eph. iv, 27: "Let not the sun go down upon your wrath, neither give place to the devil." You are loath to give place to your brother; you will say, "What, shall I yield to him?" you will not yield to him, but you will yield to him that is worse, to the devil. So you do when you yield to *wrath*.

Suppose children or servants were wrangling one with another, were not this an argument for them to be quiet, Your father is here? Your master is come? Will not all be hushed presently? God is come among us, we may see the face of God in what he hath done for us, and shall we be quarrelling before his face?

We were not without some fears lest God should leave us in the work, which some years back was begun; but now God speaks aloud to encourage us, he tells us he owns the work. Now what doth this require of us? A little logic will draw the consequence. Hath God declared himself, that he intends to go on in this work he hath begun? then let us all join together to further it to the uttermost we can; let us not exasperate the spirits of one another in ways of strife and opposition, but let every one set his hand and heart to this work, that he may be able to say, O Lord God, thou that knowest the secrets of all hearts, knowest that upon this great mercy of thine, my heart was so moved that whatever I could possibly see to be thy will, for the furtherance of this great work, as far as I was able, I did set myself to do it, and am resolved to spend my strength and life in it. If every one *did* thus, O what glory might God have from this mercy of his!

When the Lord comes to us with mercies, he expects we should rejoice in them, and sing praise; but how can we sing without harmony? Prayer requires an agreement. Matt. xviii, 18: "If two of you shall agree on earth touching anything they shall ask, it shall be done for them." Surely praise requires agreement much more. Psalms out of tune are harsh to the ear; disagreement of heart is much more so to the Spirit of God.

Surely when God hath done so much for us, it must be acknowledged to be our duty to study what sacrifice would be best pleasing to him: some sacrifice we must offer. If there be any more acceptable to him than other, surely he deserves it. If a friend had done some real kindness for you, you would be glad to know what might be most grateful to him, wherein you might testify your thankfulness. Is this in your hearts? Do you now say, "O that we did but know the thing that would be most pleasing to God; what sacrifice would be the sweetest in his nostrils! The Lord knows we would offer it freely, whatever it be." I will tell you: "That we would lay aside our divisions, our frowardness; that we would abandon all contention and strife; that we would put on bowels of mercies, kindness, humbleness of mind, meekness, long-suffering, forbearing one another, forgiving one another, if any have a quarrel against any, even as Christ forgave you, even so do ye." Col. iii, 12. "A meek and quiet spirit is, in the sight of God, of great price." 1 Pet. iii, 4. "The sacrifice of God," that which is instead of all sacrifices, "is a broken spirit." Our hearts have been broken one from another, in our unhappy divisions; O that they could break one toward another, in love and tenderness! Here would be a sacrifice more esteemed of God, than thousands of rams, and ten thousand rivers of oil: "Loving mercy, and walking humbly," is preferred before such sacrifices. Micah vi, 8.

God shows that he can own us, notwithstanding all our infirmities; why should not we own our brethren, not-withstanding their infirmities? Why should our divisions cause us to cast off one another, seeing our divisions have not provoked God to cast us off? We had need to take heed of breaches, lest God should be provoked to change his administrations toward us.

All those who are of gracious and peaceable spirits, should consider this, and go to all they know to have been at a distance one from another, with whom they have hope to do good, and seek to mollify their spirits, — to know what it is they have one against another; what prejudices, what hard thoughts, have been entertained by them, and strive by all means to remove them; that so, we, loving and delighting in one another, the Lord may love us, and delight in us, and show mercy unto us yet more and more.

Rigidness a Dividing Distemper.

Rigid, harsh, sour, crabbed, rough-hewn spirits, are unfit for union; there is no sweetness, no amiableness, no pleas-ingness in them: they please themselves in a rigid austereness, but are pleasing to none else: in their ways, they will abate nothing of their own, nor yield anything to others. This is against the rule of the apostle: "We must not please ourselves, but let every one please his neighbour, for his good to edification; and this according to the example of Christ, who pleased not himself." This is the duty, not of weak men only, who had need please others, because they have need of them, but those that are strong ought not to please themselves, but seek to please others. Men who are of austere spirits, affecting gravity which turns to a dull, sullen sternness, think it to be the commendation of the strength of their spirits, that they can carry themselves as they do toward others, seeking altogether content to themselves, without any yieldableness to others; "no, that is but lightness, and weakness in men; they are of a more staid, strong temper, than to do so." These men by their wisdom do very much sin against the wisdom of the Holy Ghost in the Scripture; yea, and against the example of Jesus Christ, who in his whole course manifested tenderness, gentleness, affableness, amiableness toward weak ones, who were infinitely beneath him: and here is set forth to us one who pleased not himself, and so was far from this rigid, harsh temper: those swords are not of the best-tempered metal which will not bend, but stand stiff; but such as yield and bend with the most ease, and stand straight again: neither are those dispositions best, which are the stiffest; but such as are most flexible, and yet stand straight too. This harsh and rigid spirit makes men's gifts and graces to be very unuseful. When Plato saw Xenocrates of an austere, rigid temper, he advised him to sacrifice to the *graces*, that he might have more mildness, fearing that otherwise his parts and learning would be unprofitable. The Jews observe upon Exod. xxv, 3, That no iron was in the stuff of the tabernacle; rigid iron spirits are very unfit for church work. Levit. xvii, 7: "They shall no more sacrifice to devils." The word translated devils, signifies rough ones; devils had their names from thence; this is the name of a satyr, Isa. xxxiv, 14, *the rough one*. The spirit of God is a dove-like, sweet spirit; but the spirit of the devil is a rough, harsh spirit, the spirit of a satyr. Prov. xi, 17: "He that is cruel troubleth his own flesh." That word here translated cruel, the Septuagint elsewhere translates by a word that signifies rigid, stiff. Men of such tempers are very troublesome to themselves, to their families, to all with whom they converse. If a smith would join two pieces of iron, he must first beat them smooth: if the joiner would join two pieces of wood, he must plain them. Except our spirits be beaten smooth, or plained, they are unfit for joining.

Rashness a Dividing Distemper.

Acts xix, 36: "Ye ought to be quiet, and do nothing rashly." Doing things rashly is opposed to quietness.

RASHNESS makes men engage themselves suddenly in business before they have examined it well. This causes much trouble, for if a man be engaged, he lies under a temptation to go on in it; as 2 Chron. xxv, 9, when the man of God came to Amaziah, to take him off from a business he was engaged in; "O but, says he, what shall I do for the hundred talents I have given out already?" Thus many answer to the truth of God, that would take them off from what they have engaged in, "But what shall I do for my credit that lies engaged?"

RASHNESS causes men suddenly to provoke others; whereas, did they consider what ill consequences might come of it, they would forbear. Rash men quickly take hold of the sword of justice to hack and hew: they think that what they do is according to reason; but they do not wisely weigh things in the balance of justice. Remember, justice hath a balance, as well as a sword. Prov. xxix, 11: "A fool uttereth all his mind." The Septuagint has it, "utters all his anger." Rash fools, by uttering all their anger, suddenly cause great stir and trouble wherever they go. The Hebrew word that signifies a fool, and that which signifies suddenly, rashly, is from the same root.

When peace sometimes is even concluded, and there is great joy, in hopes of a comfortable agreement, rashness will suddenly break it, without any due consideration.

O that that promise, Isa. lii, 4, were fulfilled among us: "The heart of the rash shall understand knowledge." Rash men presently think they understand all that can be known in such a business, and thence presume to make sudden determinations: but as over-hearty digestion causes wind, and brings much trouble to the body; so do over-hasty resolutions to men's spirits and societies.

Wilfulness a Dividing Distemper.

I think I may say, in most men, WILL is the axle-tree, lusts and passions are the wheels, whereupon almost all their actions are carried: where there is much WILL, though the thing be little about which men contend, yet the opposition may be great; as a little stone, thrown with a strong arm, may make deep impression. It is a dangerous thing to have men's wills engaged in matters of difference: it is easier to deal with twenty men's reasons, than with one man's WILL: a man of a wilful stout spirit, stands as a stake in the midst of a stream, lets all pass by him, but he stands where he was: what hope can there be of union, where there will be no yielding? One man's will raises another's; set WILL to WILL, they may dash one against another, but are not like to close, to get into one another. A wilful man thinks it beneath a wise man to alter his way; yea, it may be he thinks it a dishonour to the truth, that both he, his profession, and the honour of God, shall suffer by it. When a stubborn self-willedness is taken for a right constancy and settledness, it is very strong in men: but let us take heed of this, it is no matter though we go back from our former assertions, so long as we go forward to the truth.

Luther was called an apostate; "I am so," says he; "but it is from error to truth." Many times stoutness of spirit comes from weakness, rather than strength: there is not always the greatest strength of judgment where there is the greatest strength of will. As a man's judgment that is without prejudice is very strong, so a man's prejudice that is without judgment is as strong. The dullest horses are not always the most easily reined. "I know, and am persuaded," says the apostle. Rom. xiv, 14. Many men are persuaded before they know; those who are persuaded before they know, will not be persuaded to know. Men's WILLS will not suffer their understandings to consider: if they do consider, they will not suffer them to be convinced: if they be convinced, they will not suffer them to acknowledge that they are convinced.

Unconstancy a Dividing Distemper.

Unconstancy is evil, and a cause of division. *Stoutness* is evil, and a cause of division. A man must not be one thing one day, and another another day; not like a weathercock, carried up and down with every wind: neither must he be wilful and stout; not like a rusty lock that will not be stirred by any key. 1st. True constancy and settledness of spirit are got by much prayer and humiliation before the Lord. "Establish me, Lord, with thy free spirit; unite my heart to fear thy name" — after thy heart-breakings and meltings, and heart-cryings and pourings forth, "Lord, show me what thy will is in this thing; keep me from miscarrying; let me not settle upon any error instead of the truth; but what is thy truth, fasten my soul in it; that whatever temptations come, I may never be taken off from it" Tell God in prayer what the thing is, and what hath persuaded thy heart to embrace it; open thy heart fully to God in all thy aims; and if by this means the heart be fixed, now it is delivered from fickleness, and not fallen into stoutness.

2ndly. Where true constancy is attained, by the Spirit of God, and not by the stoutness of thine own, there is exercise of much grace, and growing up in grace, as faith, humility, love, meekness, patience, &c. 2 Peter iii, 17, 18: "Take heed ye fall not from your steadfastness; but grow in grace, and in the knowledge of our Lord and Saviour Jesus Christ." Hearts stout and wilful are dry and sapless. If the more a man hath to do with God, the more settled he is in his way; and when he hath the most full converse and sweetness of communion with God, he is then the most fully settled, satisfied, established in such a truth, which he conceived to be of God— he is safe. Many men are very stiff, and wilfully immoveable. When they have to deal with men they seem then to be the most confident men in the world; but God knows, and their conscience knows, when they solemnly set themselves in the presence of God, and have the most real sight of God, and have to deal most immediately with him, then they have misgiving thoughts; they have fears that things may not prove so sure, as they bore others in hand they apprehended them to be: but if God's presence, and thy dealings with him, confirm thee in this, thy conscience may give thee an assurance, that as thou art not fickle and wavering, so not stout and wilful.

3dly. When there is a proportion in men's constancy: if a man be resolute and constant in one thing, but very fickle and easy turned aside in others, there is cause to suspect his constancy is rather from stiffness than from grace; for grace works proportionably through the whole soul, and in the whole course of a man's life.

4thly. If the more real the presence of death and judgment appear to a man, the more settled he is in that way; this likewise may be a good evidence to him, that his settledness in such a way is right.

A Spirit of Jealousy a Dividing Distemper.

"Envy, strife, railings, evil surmisings." 1 Tim. vi, 4. Strife and evil surmisings are near of kin. If contentious men can get nothing against their brethren, they will surmise there is something. If they can find nothing in their actions to judge, they will judge their hearts. If there be nothing above-board, they will think there may be something under-board; and from thinking there may be something, they will think it very likely there is something; and from likely there is, they will conclude there is, "surely there is some plot working." But this is against the law of love, for *it thinketh no evil*; all the good that they see in their brethren, is blasted by their *suspicion* of evil. Love would teach us rather by what appears to judge the best of what appears not, than by what appears not, to judge the worst of what appears.

A Spirit of Contention a Dividing Distemper.

As in some there is a strong inclination, a vehement *impetus*, to whoredom, which the prophet calls the spirit of whoredom; so there is in others a vehement, strong disposition of heart to *contention*. These have a *spirit of contention*: they are like *salamanders*, who love, and live in the fire. They thirst after the waters of Massah and Meribah; their temper is such, as if they drank no other drink than what was brewed of those waters, *contentions* and *strifes*; so, what are as tedious to other men as death, are their delight. They are most in their element, when they are over head and ears in them. A *contentious spirit* will always find matter for contention. Prov. xxvi, 21: "As coals to burning coals, and wood to fire, so is a contentious man to kindle strife:" they are ready to put their hands to any strife they meet with; yet, "he that meddleth with strife belonging not to him, is like one that holdeth a dog by the ears." Prov. xxvi, 17. Many men have no mettle in anything but contentions. Like many jades who are dull in travel, they have mettle only to kick and to play jadish tricks. If thou hast any spirit, any zeal and courage, it is a pity it should be laid out in quarrels: reserve it for the cause of God, to strengthen thee in contending for the truth and the public good.

2.
Practices that Divide

Associating with Whisperers a Dividing Practice.

MANY MEN OF MODERATE spirits, if let alone, yet meeting with men who tell them stories, and speak ill of those men that heretofore they had a good opinion of, before they have examined what the truth is, there is a venom got in their spirits. Before they are aware, their hearts begin to be hot, and to rise against those men of whom they hear such things. Their thoughts are altered concerning them; their spirits alienated; breaches are made; and men who are innocent wonder from whence all come. O take heed of these men of evil tongues! Saint Augustine could not endure such guests at his table, and therefore caused these two lines to be writ over his table: it were well they were over some of yours:

> To speak ill of the absent forbear,
> Or do not sit at table here.

Needless Disputes a Dividing Practice.

When men have got a little knowledge, they think it is a fine thing to be arguing and disputing in matters of religion: unnecessary disputes are their necessary practice, for they shall be accounted as nobody, if they have not something to object against almost everything; but in this way of theirs they shall be accounted knowing men, men who have an insight into things, who understand more than ordinary men do: hence they turn all their religion into *disputes*, and by them they grow giddy. Wine is good in its proper place and use, but when it fumes all up into the head, it makes it giddy. Knowledge is good when the strength of it gets to the heart, to comfort it, there to breed good spirits, for the strengthening it in the ways of holiness; but when it flies all up into the head, it fills it with thousands of fancies: it causes pride and giddiness. Disputes draw the best spirits from the heart, by which they weaken it. It is a very ill sign in a man to have a contradicting spirit; to get into a vein of disputing against anything, though it be good. I have read of Gregory Nazianzen, that he told his friends that Julian would prove to be a notoriously wicked man: he gave his reason, because he took such delight in disputing against that which was good. Disputes are seldom without much heart-distemper. If they continue long, they cause snarling one at another: and no marvel though those who snarl so often, do bite at last. A man shows most parts in the *matter* of truth, but most grace in the *manner* of handling it with reverence, holiness, and modesty. Rom. xiv, 1: "Receive not the weak in faith to doubtful disputations." Here is a direct injunction against those disputes I am speaking of. Let no man say every truth is precious, the least truth is of more worth than our lives; we must contend for every truth. The least truth is so precious, that we must rather lose our lives than deny it. You must do and suffer much to maintain truth, but this in an orderly way.

First, you must be grounded in the main fundamentals of religion: you must be strong in the faith, and after that labor to edify yourselves in all the truths of God, so as one may be helpful to another. It is not for every one, who hath but little time, little knowledge, little means, little strength, to tire out himself and others in doubtful disputes. The Scripture is so much against this, as nothing can be more. 1 Tim. i, 4: "Which minister questions rather than edifying." To ask and discourse of questions about the great things that concern thy soul, thy eternal state, how thou mayest live further to the honor of God, is good, when you meet together: to confer one with another what God hath done for your souls, to tell each other the experiences of your own hearts, and God's dealings with you; what temptations you meet with, and how God helps you against them.

Such things as these would edify. But when your questions are about things you are never likely to understand; and if you did understand, they little concern you, they would not be helpful to you one whit in the ways of godliness: in these the Holy Ghost would not have you spend your time. Eccles. vii, 29: "Man was made upright, and he hath found out to himself many inventions." "Miscuerit se infinitis questionibus." So the old Latin reads it, he hath mingled himself in infinite questions. If we had but that great question more among us, What shall we do to be saved? it would cause many unprofitable questions to vanish. Never such ignorance came upon the Christian world, as in that age when the schoolmen were in the highest esteem. All religion then was turned into questions, and both the mystery and the power of godliness were lost. The things of religion are rather to be believed than disputed.

We believe fishermen, not logicians, says Ambrose. The devil at this day seeks to darken the glory of religion this way: — He sees so much light hath broke forth, that he cannot get men presently off it by profaneness, therefore he labours to eat out the strength of it, by busying them, and getting them to delight in multitudes of questions, and that about things of lesser concernment. 1 Tim. vi, 4: "He is proud and knoweth nothing, but doating about questions, and strife of words, whereof cometh envy, strife, railings, evil surmisings, perverse disputings of men of corrupt minds, and destitute of the truth. These men conceit they have more knowledge than other men; but the Holy Ghost saith they know nothing. They cry out much of the truth, and they contend for the truth; but the Holy Ghost saith they are destitute of the truth. 2 Tim. ii, 22, 23: "Follow charity and peace, but foolish and unlearned questions avoid, knowing that they do gender strifes: but the servant of the Lord must not strive." And Titus iii, 8, 9: "This is a faithful saying, and these things I will that thou affirm constantly, that they which have believed in God might be careful to maintain good works. These things are profitable unto men. But avoid foolish questions and genealogies, and contentions and strivings about the law; for they are unprofitable and vain."

The question about the law, whether a man be justified by it, or by free grace in Christ, is not one of those foolish questions and needless strivings. This is a great question, for which we are to contend; for our life is in it. But there are other questions about the law, which cause striving, rather than edifying. Let these two things be granted about the law: first, that we are not justified by it, but by the free grace of God in Christ; secondly, that what duties of holiness are set down in the law, we are bound to them by the most strong obligations. What need we contend further about the law? Let us be established in these two, and it will be sufficient for our edifying. It is likely, when Paul wrote this Epistle to Titus, the heads of the people were troubled about some such kind of questions about the law as are among us; therefore, says he, "avoid foolish questions, and strivings about the law." But now the questions about the law are driven on to such a dangerous issue, that we have cause not only to be careful to avoid them, but even to tremble at the thought of them. It is now accounted a legal thing against the grace of the gospel to confess sin, to be humbled for sin, to make conscience of duty, or to be troubled in conscience for neglect of it. No, they thank God they are delivered from such things. In respect of God, whether they sin or not, it is all one. Yea, these things prevail with those who have been forward in a profession of religion; who seemed to walk strictly, but now are grown loose. That faith is easily wrought which teacheth men to believe well of themselves, though their lives be ill. There is a mighty change in men's spirits now from that which was heretofore. Times have been, when any opinion that tended to looseness was presently disgustful and unsavoury, and rejected by such who made profession of religion.

Slaiden, in the tenth book of his commentaries, says the devil that sought to do mischief at Munster, was not a skilful devil, but rude and simple, because he sought to prevail by tempting men to looseness; whereas, says he, if he had been a cunning devil, he would rather have deceived by abstaining from flesh, by abhorring matrimony, by shows of wonderful lowliness of mind, &c. He might sooner have taken men this way. But truly now the most cunning devil sees it to be the best way to attain his ends, to raise up and foment opinions that tend to the liberty of the flesh, so that by it he can carry them on under the colour of magnifying free grace: he finds that these things are exceeding suitable to men's spirits in these times; that they are taken in by such who formerly appeared so conscientious, that he feared he should never have been able to have prevailed with them. He never found a way like to this to prevail with such men; yea, never a way like to this to choke the word, when it first begins to work upon the heart. He hath blasted more young converts this way, than ever he did by any way since he was a devil. Heretofore the way was to stir up others to deride them for following the word, and for praying; but now he hath a way worth two of that, to make them to deride others for their conscientiousness in following the word and praying; and this strengthened with a high persuasion that hereby they are the great magnifiers of the free grace of God in the gospel— the only men who understand the gospel way. This devil now looks upon himself and his fellows as simple and foolish in all their former devices. Here is an experiment beyond them all; seeing this, Christ must needs be magnified, he will magnify him too. Seeing the gospel must go on, he will put it on too. He will find out a device here, to strike at the practice, power, and life of godliness, in a more secret and prevailing way than ever formerly was done. It is likely in this generation the former principles of godliness will not be got out: but if this way prevails still in proportion to what it hath done, in a generation or two it is likely to bring general profaneness and licentiousness upon the face of the Christian world more than any way of Satan ever since the world began; for here is a way to be loose and profane, and to satisfy conscience too.

Not Keeping Within the Bounds that God hath Set, A Dividing Practice.

First, then, when men will be meddling with that which concerns them not; that is out of their sphere. 1 Thess. iv. 11: "Study to be quiet, and do your own business." Prov. xx, 31: "It is an honour for a man to cease from strife; but every fool will be meddling." When *manna* was gathered, and kept in that proportion God would have it, it was very good; but when men must have more, and keep it longer than God would have them, then it bred worms. Thus it will be in all that we have or do. Let us keep the proportion God sets us, and all will be well; but if we think to provide better for ourselves, by going beyond our measure, worms are presently bred in all.

Peter Martyr, in an epistle to the ministers and such as professed the faith in Polonia, exhorts them to endeavour the establishing of discipline in the church as soon as they could, while people's hearts were heated with love to and desires after the gospel. He tells them it will be harder to bring it in afterward, when their hearts begin to grow more cold. And that they might not think discipline a small thing, he says that those churches cannot be said to profess the gospel truly, nor solidly, which want it. He would have them consider it not to be the least part of the Christian religion; and to know that the gospel is neglected by such as shall put off from themselves such a singular, excellent portion of it. But, says he, this will be the objection, under the colour of discipline, the ministers will tyrannize; they will carry things according to their minds.

Propagating Evil Reports, A Dividing Practice.

This may be done, you know, otherwise than by the tongue; and this hath been an old dividing way. If we can blast the chief of a party, we shall do well enough with the rest; therefore let us make as ill interpretations of what they do as we possibly can. Let us fasten as ill things upon them as we can have any colour or pretence for. Let reports be raised, fomented, and spread: whether they be true or no, it makes no matter, something will stick. Jer. ii, 10: "Report, say they, and we will report it;" do but raise a report— let us be able to say we heard it, or there was a letter written about such a thing, and we will boldly assert it: the apprehension of it will prevail with many; however, these men shall not have that esteem in their hearts, as generally as heretofore they have had; and if we once get down their esteem, we shall do well enough with their cause. If we can meet with any bold spirit that will venture to encounter with them in this; that will dare to take upon him to gather up, or make, or aggravate, or wrest reports; or do anything that may render them otherwise in the thoughts and hearts of men than hitherto they have been; we shall break them. It is but one or two venturing the hard thoughts of men to make an experiment: some may be found fit for such a business; we will find out ways to encourage them. If their hearts begin to fail, we will apply warm clothes to them, we will one way or other support them. This must be done, or else whatsoever we do will be to no purpose. Something or other must be found to serve our ends in this. Doth Moses prevail too much in the hearts of the people? Something must be found against him. If we can find nothing against himself, yet will we find something against his wife. *She is an Ethiopian woman.* Num. xii, 1. And yet, who was she but the daughter of Jethro, to whom he had been married many years before? for an Ethiopian and Midianitish woman were all one. But now we are resolved to pick out whatever we can get information of, though it be in things done many years since, when they lived in such or such places, in times of old: it will serve our turn; we may fasten it upon them. Prov. xvi, 27: "An ungodly man diggeth up evil, and in his lips there is a burning fire." If he hath nothing above ground, he will dig something up, though it be, both what by God and man hath been buried long since. David was a public instrument of God for much good; yet (Psa. xxxi, 11,) "he was a reproach among his enemies, but especially among his neighbours." Nehemiah raised by God for great service, what dirt was cast upon him? he was accused of sedition and rebellion. Paul a pestilent fellow — he and his company with him, turned the world upside down; what evil can be devised, but was fastened upon the Christians in the primitive times? They charge them as being the cause of all their misery. If they have ill weather; if the rivers overflow; if Nilus does not flow; if there be an earthquake, plague, famine; hale the Christians to the lions. At their meetings they said they made *Thyestes* suppers, who invited his brother to a supper, and presented him a dish of his own flesh, a limb of his son! Many such abominable things were fastened upon them, as are not fit to be named. Tertullian tells the Christians, that they were *funambulones*, like men upon a rope: if they went one step awry, they were in danger to be undone by it; so narrowly did their enemies watch them, and so malicously did they aggravate all their miscarriages. Thus the most eminent after his time, as Athanasius, he was as miserably aspersed as ever poor man in this world by the Arian party. They rendered him most odius to his friends and strangers. In the beginning of the reformation the Waldenses were so aspersed, that the story says of them, there was not one arrow in the quiver of malice, but it was drawn forth and shot at them. Luther, Calvin, Beza, Oecolampadius, Bullinger, and the rest, are by some in writing rendered the most black and vile pieces that the earth bore, both in their lives and deaths. I find it recorded by Zuinglius, that he was a man so eminent, that his friends made him almost a God; and so traduced by his enemies, that one would wonder the earth did not open and swallow up such a man.

As for the servants of God, they commit their names and ways to God, knowing that the Lord takes care of their names as well as their souls. If dirt be cast upon a mud wall it sticks; but if upon marble, it soon washes or moulders away. God will in time justify his servants, even in your consciences, by the constancy of their peaceable carriage toward men, and their gracious, holy walking, with their God. Only take you heed that you involve not yourselves in the guilt of that wrong that is done unto them, by the readiness of your spirits to close with, and take content in, what evil you hear of those whom God accounts faithful.

An Inordinate Cleaving to Some, so as Denying Due Respect to Others, A Dividing Practice.

This was the practice among the Corinthians which caused great divisions among them. Some were of Paul, some of Apollos, some of Cephas. No question a man may in his heart more reverence and prize, and outwardly show more respect to, those whom God makes the greatest instruments of good, (caeteris paribus) than to others. David showed more respect to Nathan than to Gad. Nathan was by far more intimate with him: the intimacy was such between them, that Nathan thought it a very strange thing that David should do anything about the disposing of his crown, and not make him acquainted with it. So Valentinian the emperor honoured Ambrose above any of the bishops in his time. Such men as God is not pleased to make so instrumental for good as others, should not envy this: let them be willing that those should be honoured whom God honours: but yet people should take heed that they give not so much honour to one that they deny due respect to others. And ministers, and others in public places, should not entertain, much less seek for or rejoice in, any honour or respect given to them, which they see detracts from that esteem and countenance that are due to others. The weakness and folly of people in their inordinate giving, or denying respect, are often caused, but more ordinarily fomented and increased, by the pride and vanity of teachers, in seeking for, or at least in a pleasing embracing of, such inordinate respect given to them, whereby others suffer much. Siding of parties is made, and more hurt comes to the public, than their honours are worth a thousand times over. This evil many times comes of it, that reason and truth from one man are little regarded, and error and weakness from another man as greedily embraced, and stiffly maintained: whereas it should be with reason and truth, as it is with money: one man's money in a market is as good as another's; so should one man's reason and truth, spoken by him, be as good as another's.

Because Men Cannot Join in All Things with Others, They will Join in Nothing, A Dividing Practice.

Some men are of such dividing dispositions, that if they be offended with a man in any one thing, in hearing or otherwise, they will go away in a touchy mood, resolving never to hear him more. You think you have liberty in any froward mood to cast off that means of good which God offers to you; to partake of such men's gifts and graces as you please. It may be, your stomach is so high and great on a sudden, or your spirit is fallen into such a sullen humour, that you will not so much as go or send to him, to see, if, upon a serious and quiet examination of things, you may not have satisfaction in what for the present offends. No men's spirits are carried on with such present, rash, heady resolutions. I believe there was never such a kind of spirit prevailing among such as profess godliness, since the Christian religion was in the world. Never did so many withdraw from hearing, even those by whom they acknowledge God hath spoken to their hearts; and that before they have gone to them, to impart what it is that scruples them, to try whether they may not get some satisfaction. Certainly, if you have no need of the word, the word hath no need of you. You may easily express your discontents one to another; you may easily say you are resolved you will never hear such a one any more; but you cannot so easily answer this to Jesus Christ. When your weaknesses, the prevailing of your distempers, shall grate upon your consciences, this will be a great aggravation of the evil of them; you neglected in a humoursome way, and self-willed resolution, those means that might have done your soul good, even such as many hundreds, if not thousands of souls, bless God for, all the days of their lives, yea, are now blessing God in heaven for. Heretofore you would have been glad of that which now you slight and reject. This is not from more light or strength that you have now, but from more vanity.

To Commend and Countenance What We Care Not For, In Opposition to What We Dislike, A Dividing Practice.

When such as profess godliness, shall make much of wicked men; shall commend them, join with them, embrace them, yea, be well pleased with the bitterness, boisterousness, and boldness, of their daring spirits, because there may be use made of them, against those men and ways they differ from; this is an evil which brings guilt upon themselves, and makes the division between them and their brethren very great. If your hearts be right, and your cause be good, you need not make use of anything that is evil, to comfort your hearts, or to maintain your cause. The Lord will not be beholden to the evil, the bitterness of men's spirits, for the furtherance of his cause; and why should you? God will not take the wicked by the hand; neither shouldest thou. Why do you seek to strengthen yourselves by stirring up vile men to join with you; such as heretofore your hearts were opposite to? How comes it to pass you can close so lovingly now? You can smile one upon another, and shake hands together. How comes it to pass you do rejoice the hearts of evil men; they encourage you, and you encourage them? Those unsavoury, bitter expressions, that come from them you can smile at and be well pleased with, because they are against such as differ from you. Blow up that sparkle of ingenuity that heretofore hath been in you. Lay your hands upon your hearts, bethink yourselves, Is it the Spirit of Jesus Christ that actuates us in such a way wherein we are? Surely this is not the way of peace, but of division and confusion.

Revenge, A Dividing Practice.

When any provoke you, you say you will be even with him. There is a way whereby you may be not even with him, but above him; that is, forgive him. Practising revenge is the way to continue divisions to the end of the world. Such offend me, therefore I will offend them; and therefore they offend me again, and I them, and so it may run *in infinitum*. They deny me a kindness, therefore I will deny them, and therefore they will deny me; so these unkindnesses run on endlessly. Divisions will have a line of succession. Where will it, where can it stop, if this be the way of men?

A gentleman of very good credit, who lived at court many years, told me, that himself once heard a great man in the kingdom say he never forgave a man in his life: and I am moved the rather to believe it to be so, because I have been told by some other gentlemen, that the same man would, when he was walking alone, speak to himself, and clap his hands upon his breast, and swear by the name of God, that "he would be revenged, he would be revenged." And that she who lay in his bosom was wont to sit alone and sing to herself, "Revenge! revenge! how sweet is revenge!"

Part II
The Evils of Divisions.

What heart that hath any tenderness in it bleeds not in the sense of these sore and dreadful heart divisions there are among us? The evil there is in them is beyond what tongue or pen can express. Take a view of it under these two heads. 1st. The good they hinder. 2d. The sin they cause.

1.

The Good They Hinder.

First. The Quiet, Comfort, and Sweetness of Our Spirits, Are Hindered by Divisions.

THEY PUT THE SPIRIT out of tune: men who have heretofore had sweet spirits full of ingenuity, since they have interested themselves in these divisions, have lost their sweetness, their ingenuity is gone. When the bee stings, she leaves her sting behind her, and never gathers honey more. Men by stinging one another, do not lose their stings, but they lose their honey; they are never like to have that sweetness in their hearts that heretofore they had. "Shall I lose my sweetness," says the fig-tree, "and go to be promoted over the trees?" Why dost thou not reason thus with thy spirit? Shall I lose my sweetness in contending to get my will, to be above others? God forbid! There was a time that both myself and others found much sweetness in the temper of our spirit. There was nothing but peaceableness, quiet, calmness, contentedness, in it: and how comfortable was such a temper of spirit! Methought, when my spirit was in that sweet frame, all things were sweet to me; but since I have been interested in quarrels and contentions it hath been far otherwise. Prov. xv, 4. Perverseness in the tongue causes a breach in the spirit. Contentions cause much perverseness in men's tongues, and this causes a breach in their spirits. Your contending costs you dear. Though it were in nothing else, yet the loss of this sweetness of spirit makes it very costly to you. All the wrong that you should have put up if you had not contended, had not been so great an evil to you as this one thing is. There is nothing more contrary to ingenuity than quarrelsomeness. It is reported of Melancthon, that when he was to die he had this speech, and Stringelius at his death had the same: "I desire to depart this life for two causes; first, that I may enjoy the desired sight of the Son of God, and the church in heaven. Secondly, that I may be delivered from the fierce and implacable hatred of divines." There was much disputing, contending, quarrelling, in those times, which was so tedious to the spirits of those good men, as it made them the more willing to die, that they might be where their souls should be at rest. That saint of God, old Mr. Dodd, never loved to meddle with controversies; he gave this reason, he found his heart the worse when he did. Men seldom come away from hot disputes, or any other contentions, but their spirits are altered for the worse. They find it so, and others find it in them. If a man has been abroad, and met with company with whom he hath been contending, his wife, children, servants, find that he comes not home with the same spirit that he went out with.

Secondly. They Hinder the Freedom of a Man's Spirit, Which a Wise Man Sets a High Price Upon.

The strength of many men's spirits is spent in contentions. They have no command of them in anything else. When a man is once engaged in a contest, he knows not how to get off. Contention is a great snare to a man: he wishes he had never meddled with it; he is weary of it: but knows not how to come off fairly. We read of Moses (Deut. xxxiv, 7) that he was a hundred and twenty years old when he died; his eye was not dim, nor his natural force abated. Some give this to be one reason of such a wonderful preservation of his health and strength, the meekness of his spirit. God witnesses of him, (Num. xii, 3,) that he was the meekest man upon the face of the earth.

Thirdly. They Hinder the Sweetness of Christian Converse and Communion.

You know your communion with the saints was wont to be far more sweet than now it is. Ye were wont to have your hearts spring at the sight of one another: *Ipse aspectus boni viri delectat*, says Seneca. The very sight of a good man delights. The sight of a godly man was wont to delight us otherwise than now it does. You look one upon another now sourly, with lowering countenance, and withdraw from one another. Your comforts were wont to be double, treble, sevenfold, a hundredfold, according to that society of saints you conversed withal. One godly man accounted it the joy of his heart that he had anything that he could communicate to another godly man, and the other had the like joy that he had anything to communicate to him. Thus comforts were multiplied. But now your comforts are single. O the sweetness, the suitableness, there were wont to be in the spirits of Christians! Shall I say suitableness? It was blessed oneness of heart.

They did as it were exchange souls one with another every day. Their souls did close clasp one with, and cleave one to, another! O how did they love to open their heart one to another! What delight was there in pouring forth their spirits into one another! What cheerfulness was there wont to be in their meeting! They eat their bread together with singleness of heart and joy, praising the Lord. There were no such cheerful meetings in the world, as the meetings of the saints were wont to be. They parted one from another with their souls bound up one in another: their hearts warmed, enlarged, resolved, strengthened, in God's ways. But now they cannot meet together but they fall a jarring, contending one with another, and part with spirits estranged from, soured, and imbittered one against another; their hearts weakened, and more unsettled in the things of God than before. Heretofore when they were absent one from another, yet the remembrance one of another was joyful. But these days seem to be gone. Where is there that opening of secrets one to another as formerly? Every one is afraid of another. What sweet visits were there wont to be! What bearing one another's burdens! What heart-encouraging letters! It was with the saints as in Tertullian's time, Christians called one another brethren, and were ready to die for one another. But now these are opposed to one another's spirits: they bring evil upon one another.

Fourthly. They Hinder Our Time.

Abundance of time is spent about our divisions, which we are not able to give account to God for. When men are engaged in contentions, they will follow them night and day: whatever business be neglected, to be sure that must not. Yea, the choice of our time, that was wont to be spent in meditation, reading, prayer, is now spent in contending and wrangling. Those retired times that we were wont to converse with God in, are now spent in the workings of our own thoughts about divisions; and when we come abroad, then a great part of our time is given up in going, first to this body, and then to the other, to help forward and foment matter of division. Of all the time of a man's life, that time that is spent in lawing and quarrelling is the worst; and happy it were for many, that it might not be reckoned among the days, weeks, or months, of their lives.

Fifthly. They Hinder Our Prayers.

"If two or three agree together touching anything they shall ask, it shall be done for them of my Father," says Christ. Matt. xviii, 19. 1 Tim. ii, 8: "I will that men pray, lifting up their hands, without wrath." When Daniel was in a strait, he goes to his companions, and desires them to lift up prayers to God for him. Dan. ii, 17. There was a sweet agreement between them; hence their stock and trade in prayer one with another. 1 Pet. iii, 7. The apostle giving rules for a peaceable, loving life, between man and wife. The woman must be meek, and the man live with his wife as a man of knowledge; and they must walk together as the heirs of life. Why so? "That your prayers may not be hindered." Private contentions in families are great hinderances of family prayers: so our public divisions and contentions are the great hinderance of the prayers of Christians in a more public way. How were they wont to pour forth their hearts in prayer together! but now it is otherwise. Men do not now walk together as the heirs of life; therefore their prayers are hindered. God accepts not of our gift, if we offer it when our hearts are at a distance from our brethren. When breaches continue, and we are not reconciled, you know Christ requires us to leave our gift at the altar, till reconciliation be made. It is the Spirit of God in the saints that is the spirit of prayer: now God's Spirit is a dove-like, meek, quiet, and peaceable spirit.

Sixthly. They Hinder the Use of Our Gifts.

When vessels are soured with vinegar, they spoil liquor that is poured into them; they make it good for nothing. Many men have excellent gifts, but they are in such sour, vinegar spirits, that they are of little or no use in church and commonwealth.

1. In these times of division, many men exercise their gifts and parts in little or nothing else but in matters of division. Do you think that God hath given you such parts for no other end but this?

2. They have no hearts to impart to their brethren their gifts, in counselling, admonishing, strengthening, and comforting; no, their hearts are estranged from them, they care not to have anything to do with them. But do you think you are so far your own men, that you may keep in or employ your talents as you please? Are you not the stewards of Christ? Are they not given to you for the edification of your brethren, as well as for good to yourselves? Can this satisfy your consciences? Such a one differs from you; he hath angered you; therefore though you have opportunity of being useful to him, yet you refuse it, as if it were at your liberty to lay out your abilities for good, or not: certainly this is not according to the mind of Christ. 1 Cor. xii, 7: "The manifestation of the Spirit is given to every man to profit withal."

3. If you do make use of your gifts for the good of others, yet dissensions between you will hinder the profit of them. You are not like to do any good by them. Except they be carried on by the oil of love, they will not soak into men's hearts. When did you ever know a wrangling, contentious minister, (though his gifts were never so excellent,) do good among his people? And what comfort can a man have of his life, if he be laid aside by God as a useless man?

4. These divisions cause men to make the gifts of oth-

ers useless to themselves, whereas God puts opportunity into men's hands to get much good by those excellent gifts their brethren have; yet if there be any difference between them, either they will not acknowledge the gifts of God in them, or otherwise they have no mind to receive from them that good they might have, because their hearts are not with them.

Seventhly. They Hinder Our Graces.

How little of God and Christ, how little spiritualness in professors of religion, since these rents and divisions have been among us, in comparison of what in former times hath appeared! "As the members of the body," says Augustine, "are not quickened, except they be joined, so even the members of Christ do not receive of the quickening virtue of Christ, except they be joined." Here is the reason of the deadness, coldness, emptiness, barrenness, vanity of your spirits, you are not joined. O where are the heavenly Christians that were wont to be— those humble, those holy, gracious souls, who lived by faith, who were able to deny themselves; their whole lives were nothing but a continual exercise of self-denial; who were not only patient, but joyful, under afflictions? Where are those watchful Christians who walked close with God; who enjoyed such spiritual communion with him, as made their faces shine in their holy, heavenly conversations? Where are those tender, broken-hearted Christians, that were wont to be, who lived upon the word, to whom the word was more sweet than honey and the honey-comb? Now there is another kind of professors of religion, as if godliness in these days were not of the same kind with that which was formerly. If our forefathers who were the most holy, and gracious, should rise again, they would not own those for professors of religion who now make a great noise, and keep a great stir about religion, as if they had got up higher than their forefathers had, and yet are loose, vain, frothy, false in their way. Certainly, those holy, gracious saints, whom these new professors slight, were they alive would abominate them, as the great disgrace of, and dishonour to, Jesus Christ and his saints. Our divisions hinder the breaking forth of the lustre, the shine of religion in the beauty and glory of it. The fire of our contentions raises such a smoke, that it all besmothers us; it takes away our comeliness: it makes us look black. No amiableness appears in the ways of religion to convince men of the excellency of them. Scratched faces, rent and torn garments, we account a shame to us. Distracted, divided spirits, rending and tearing one another, and from one another in our divided ways. O how uncomely doth it render us, and that profession of religion that we take upon us! The Turks were wont to wonder much at our Englishmen for pinking and cutting their clothes, counting them little better than madmen for making holes in whole cloth, which time of itself would tear too soon: the cuts, rents, slashes, that are in our spirits in our divisions, are much more uncomely, and may justly render us foolish and mad in the eyes of all that behold us. Our divisions hinder our strength. If you untwist a cable, how weak is it in the several parts of it! A threefold cord is not easily broken; but a single one is. Divide a strong current into several rivulets, and how shallow and weak will the course of the water be! They hinder our doing good in public: that which concerns many, must be done by many; but how can two, much less many, walk together, if they be not agreed? That which one does the other seeks to undo. Now, although God can turn whatever is contrary to his work to the furtherance of it, yet man cannot do so. When God would hinder the work of building Babel, he comes down and confounds their tongues, so they could not join together in it. Thus when the devil would hinder the work of Jerusalem, he knows no way more likely than by dividing the hearts of those who are employed, if he possibly can, that thereby he might bring confusion.

They hinder our own ends. None are more crossed in their ends and designs than contentious people. We have not the mutual benefit of one another's estates, houses, the many ways of accommodation and help for one another, as heretofore we were wont to have. Now every man shifts for himself; scarce any man who knew what the heartiness of friendship meant, enjoys those outward accommodations as he was wont. They hinder the blessing of God. The Psalmist commending the love of brethren, concludes: "There the Lord commanded the blessing, even life for evermore." Psalm, cxxxiii. There! that is, where the love of brethren is, there is a blessing, a blessing commanded by God; it comes with power, and this no less than life, and this life for evermore. "God dwells in Salem," says Luther, "not in Babylon: where there is peace, not where there is confusion."

Thus you see how great evil there is in our divisions, in respect to what good we lose by them. Now then consider, whether it be possible that any gain we can get by them can recompense this loss. Can anything got by them quit the cost? But if it could be supposed our loss may be recompensed, yet I am sure nothing can countervail the evil there is in them, in respect of the sinfulness of them. That is the next head.

2.
The Sinfulness of our Divisions.

THOUGH THERE BE SIN in many things mentioned, yet we considered them in reference to our good that was hindered; but now let us consider what venom of sin there is in them. The number 2 hath been accounted accursed, because it was the first that parted from unity. The departure from that unity God would have, is a very cursed thing; for it hath much sin in it. That which St. Augustine says of original sin we may well apply to our divisions;— they are sin, the punishment of sin, the cause of sin, nothing but a heap of sin.

First, they are against the solemn charge and command of God, and of Jesus Christ, 1 John iii, 23: "This is his commandment, that we should believe on the name of his Son Jesus Christ, and love one another as he gave us commandment." It is not an arbitrary thing that we should love one another; but it is the command of God, and a great command joined to that of believing in his Son Jesus Christ. The one is as truly necessary to salvation as the other. Let men talk of faith, of believing on the Son of God, of trusting to free grace in Christ; yet if they have dividing, contending spirits, no love, no sweetness, no grace of union with the saints, their faith is a dead faith. And because God stands much upon this to have his people live together in love, at the beginning of the verse he says, "It is his commandment;" at the end of the verse he says, "He gave us commandment." And it is also observable, that he says of the commandment of love, that "he gave us that commandment." It is a gift, for it is a sweet commandment. We should not only submit to it, as being bound by the authority of it; but we should open our hearts to it, and embrace it joyfully as a gift of God. The commandment of love God gives us as a gift from his love. The excellency of these commandments are further amplified, verse 24: "And he that keepeth his commandments dwelleth in him, and he in him." I do not think that you can find, in all the Scripture, any command of God in one verse and a piece of another, so inculcated and commended. Again, chap. iv, 21: "This commandment have we from him, that he who loveth God loveth his brother also." If you think you have any command to love God, or to believe in Jesus Christ, know the same authority lays a command upon you, to love your brother also. John xv, 12: "This is my commandment, that ye love one another as I have loved you:" and verse 17: "These things I command you, that ye love one another." Christ, you see, likewise makes a great matter of the saints loving one another. Surely the sin, then, must needs be great that breaks such a great commandment as this, upon which God the Father, and Jesus Christ his Son, lay so much weight.

Secondly. These unkind and unloving divisions are against the prayer of Jesus Christ; yea, against that prayer he made for us a little before he died. John xvii, 21, he prayed to his Father, that all who did believe, and should after believe on him, might be one as his Father is in him, and he is in his Father, and that they "may be one in the

Father and him." As if he should say, O Father, I am now going out of the world; and I foresee, when I am gone, even those whom thou hast given me, who are one in me and in thee, will meet with strong temptations to divide them one from another. But, O Father, I beseech thee, let thy fatherly care be over them, to keep their hearts together, that they may be united in the strongest union that is possible for creatures to be united in! O Father, let them be one, as thou and I am one! Would we not be loath to lose the benefit of that heavenly prayer of Christ for us in the seventeenth of John? Read it over; see what soul-ravishing excellency there is in it, seeing he hath expressly said he intended us who live now in it, as well as those disciples who then lived with him. Let us prize this prayer, as being more to us than ten thousand worlds. Luther writes a chiding letter to Melancthon. "By those sinful, distrustful fears, and carking thoughts of yours," says he, "you do *Irritas facere præces nostras*, you make void our prayers." How great, then, is our divisions! By them we do what in us lies to make void, as concerning us, the prayer, that blessed prayer, of Jesus Christ.

Thirdly. Our divisions are very dishonourable to Jesus Christ. Were it that they darkened our names only, it were not so much; but that which darkens the glory of Jesus Christ, should go very near unto us. I have read of Alexander Severus, seeing two Christians contending one with another, commanded them that they should not presume to take the name of Christians upon themselves any longer; "For," says he, "you dishonour your Master, Christ, whose disciples you profess to be. It is a dishonour to a general to have his army routed and run into confusion." The devil seems to prevail against us in these our divisions, so as to rout us. John xvii, 21, 23, is a notable scripture to show the sinfulness of our divisions, in the dishonour they put upon Christ; and it may be as strong an argument against them as any I know in the book of

God. Christ praying to the Father for the union of his saints, uses this argument, O Father, let this be granted, " that the world may believe that thou hast sent me." And again, ver. 23: "Let them be perfect in one, that the world may know that thou hast sent me." If they be not united one to another in love and peace, but have a spirit of division ruling among them, what will the world think? Surely that thou didst not send me. That I who am their head, their teacher, and Lord, never came from thee; for thou art wisdom, holiness, and love; and if I had come from thee, then those who own me to be theirs, and whom I own to be mine, would hold forth in their conversations something of that spirit of holiness, wisdom, and love, there is in thee. But when the world does not see this in them, but the clean contrary, they will never believe that I came from thee. Those truths I came into the world to make known as from thee, O Father, will not be believed, but rather persecuted; if those who profess them, by their divisions one from another, and oppositions one against another, show forth a spirit of pride, folly, envy, and frowardness. Therefore, O Father, let them be, as thou and I am, one. If this petition be not granted, how shall I look the world in the face? I shall be contemned in the world. What, am I cut down from thee for such glorious ends as, indeed, those were for which I came into the world; and when I should come to attain those ends for which I came, shall there be such a carriage in those who do profess my name, that by it the world shall persuade themselves that thou didst never send me? O what a sore evil would this be! Surely any Christian heart must needs tremble at the least thought of having a hand in so great an evil as this is.

Fourthly. Divisions are sinful, because they grieve the Holy Spirit of God. Eph. iv, 30, 31: "Grieve not the Holy Spirit of God, whereby ye are sealed to the day of redemption." Surely there is no godly heart but will say,

"O God, forbid that I should do anything to grieve the good Spirit of God. It is the Spirit that hath enlightened me, that revealed the great mysteries of God, of Christ, of eternal life, unto me. It is that Spirit that hath drawn my soul to Jesus Christ; that hath comforted it with those consolations that are more to me than ten thousand worlds: the Spirit that hath strengthened me, that helps me against temptations, that carries me through difficulties, that enables me to rejoice in tribulations: the Spirit that hath sealed me to the day of redemption: and now shall I be guilty of so great a sin as to grieve this blessed Spirit of the Lord? If I did but know wherein I have grieved it, it could not but make my soul to bleed within me, that I should have such a wretched heart to grieve this Holy Spirit, by whom my soul hath enjoyed so much good. I hope I should for ever hereafter take heed of that thing. I would rather suffer any grief in the world to mine own spirit, than be any occasion of grief to that blessed Spirit of God." But would you know what it is that hath grieved it, and what it is that is like to grieve it further? Mark what follows, verse 31: "Let all bitterness, wrath, anger, clamour, and evil speaking, be put away from you, with all malice." And would you do that which may please the Holy Spirit? O! God knows it would be the greatest joy in the world for me to do it. Then observe verse 32: "Be ye kind one to another, tender-hearted, forgiving one another; even as God for Christ's sake hath forgiven you."

Fifthly. These divisions do grieve and offend our brethren. This should not be a light matter with us. Christ accounts it a great evil to offend one of his little ones. We may think it a little matter to give offence to some of God's people who are poor and mean in the world; so long as we have the bravery of it, and the countenance of great men, no matter for them. But, friend, whatever slight thoughts thou hast of it, Christ thinks it a great matter.

You may look upon them as under you; the times may favour you more than them: but if you shall give them cause to go to God, to make their moans to him of any ill usage they have had from you, and say, "Lord, thou knowest I was for peace to the uttermost I could, so far as I was able to see thy word for my guide; but these who heretofore were as brethren to me, now their spirits are estranged, their hearts are imbittered, their words and their carriage are very grievous, and all because I cannot come up to what their opinions, their ways are." Certainly this would prove very ill to you, regard it as lightly as you will.

It may be when others carry themselves toward you otherwise than you expected, you vent yourselves against them in quarrelling, in giving ill language, in vilifying and scorning. Your strength runs out this way: but there are a generation of men, who being wronged, improve their strength in patient bearing, yea, in making their moan to God in the exercise of faith, in committing their cause to him. In Matt. xviii, 24-31, you have the story of the servant who had ten thousand talents forgiven him, who yet took his fellow-servant by the throat, who owed him a hundred pence, and put him into prison. The text says, "When his fellow-servants saw what was done, they were sorry, and came and told their lord what was done." You do not hear them cry out of their fellow-servant, "O what a vile, base wretch, was he, who would deal thus with his fellow!" No; but they went and told their lord. It is not the way of Christians when they apprehend wrong, to give ill language, to seek to right themselves or others by bitter, provoking expressions; but their hearts being filled with grief, if they must needs vent it, if quiet debates with their brethren will not ease them, let them vent themselves in the pouring forth their complaints to the Lord.

Sixthly. There is much sin in our divisions; for they stir up much corruption on all sides, both in ourselves and others. As if you shake a glass of water that has dirt in the bottom, the dirt spreads itself all over, so doth the dirty stuff of our hearts. These divisions causing a commotion in them, those corruptions are now discovered, that neither ourselves nor others had thought had been in us. Do not say in your hearts, and it may be one to another, Who would have thought it possible that so much filthy stuff should lie so long in such men's hearts undiscovered, which now appears since these unhappy divisions have been among us? James iii, 16: "Where there is envying and strife, there is confusion, and every evil work." When snakes are cold, they lie still; but if the heat of fire comes to them, then they hiss, and put forth their stings. Thus men's corruptions heat by the fire of contention that is kindled among us, till they begin to stir, to act, yea, to rise very high. The reason that some give of that prohibition of the apostle, (Ephes. iv,) "Let not the sun go down upon your wrath;" which also I find Chrysostom upon the place gives; is this, because when men's wrath is stirred by contending, if it continue in the heat of it till night, as they lie upon their beds, their corruptions will be boiling: they will lie musing and plotting against those that contend with them; their thoughts in the night season will work up their corruptions to a great height. Have you not found it so, when the sun was gone down upon your wrath, you could hardly sleep that night? William the Conqueror, in his first year, commanded that every night, at eight o'clock, a bell should be rung, and that all people then should put out their fire, which they called the Curfew Bell. It were well if some were admonished every night to cover the fire of their passions.

We stir up likewise the corruptions of others, in these our divisions. Do you not see those distempers, formerly

mentioned, working and breaking forth in your brethren, when you provoke them in your contending with
them? O pity, pity thy brother, if thou canst not pity thyself! Does it not grieve thee that thy brother should
bring sin upon himself? Were it not better for thee to
suffer, than for thy brother to sin? It is an evil thing to
be an occasion of grief to our brethren. "The Lord does
not willingly grieve the children of men;" but to be an
occasion of sin to them is much worse. When did you
ever meet with your brethren, and had your spirits
put into any heat, but after your parting, when you
began to be cool, you then saw cause to grieve for
unbeseeming words, carriage, and breakings forth of
passion, that there was either in you or them. Sometimes in a froward debate there is more sin committed
in one hour than there is otherwise in a whole twelve-
month, between those who live lovingly and sweetly
together. Yea, sometimes such corruptions are stirred
by differences and divisions that are incompatible to a
saint; namely, the rejoicing in the evil of other men, yea,
of godly men. David said his zeal had even consumed
him, because his enemies had forgotten God's word. But
some men's zeal doth even consume them, because their
friends do remember God's word. The more inoffensively
they walk, the more are they troubled. It were endless to
mention the uncharitableness, wrong, malice, injustice,
oppression, cruelty, with the abundance of other sins, that
are caused by our divisions.

Seventhly. Yet further, as they stir up sin, so they
harden in sin, as fire hardens the clay into brick. Thus
are men's hearts hardened in evil by our divisions; men
who heretofore had tender spirits, whose hearts were
ready to relent upon any brotherly admonition; but now
they are stiff, they stand out sturdily, yea, behave themselves scornfully. O this fire of contention hath baked their
lusts, hath hardened their hearts! Ezek. xi. God promises

to give his people one heart, which should be a heart of flesh. While the hearts of the saints are united, they are tender; but when they divide, they grow hard. Hence is the reason why brethren being fallen out, it is so hard to convince either of them of any ill carriage. They are angry, and they think they do well to be angry, and all because their hearts are hardened. Jonah was in a pettish mood, and his heart was hardened with it. Let God himself come now to convince him, he stands it out, he will by no means acknowledge himself faulty:— no, what he does he will justify, he does well to be angry.

Eighthly. There is much sin in them, for they are means to keep off others from God's ways. If this be their religion, say they, for men to quarrel one with another, we will have none of it. Carnal-hearted men are apt to charge religion with all the miscarriages of the professors of it You know what Saint Paul says, 1 Cor. xiv: "If men speak with strange tongues, and there comes in one unlearned, will they not be to him as barbarians; will they not say they are mad?" Thus when the men of the world look upon those who profess religion, and see their carriage, their ways strange, and divided among themselves, will they not think them even as mad people? "I charge you," says the church, (Cant. iii, 5,) "by the roes and by the hinds, that you stir not up my beloved till he please." This by some is interpreted thus, The roes and hinds are shy and fearful creatures, and by them are signified such as are observers of the ways of the church, and ready to take offence at anything they see amiss in them: therefore I charge you, say those who are faithful, that you do nothing that may make any disturbance in the church, whereby such as are observers of your ways shall be offended. If they see miscarriages in you, they will fly off. And of all miscarriages, there are none more offensive to the lookers on than wranglings and contendings. When they see this, they will conclude, surely this is not the way of Christ.

They are a very ill improvement of our zeal and courage. Zeal and courage have such an excellency in them, that it is a thousand pities they should have no other improvement, than to raise and maintain quarrels and divisions. The Lord hath use for every man's zeal and courage. Reserve them for him, for some notable work that God hath for thee to do, and do not spend them about that from whence comes no good. If soldiers lying near their enemies, having no store of powder, should spend what they have in making squibs and fire-works, would they not be condemned of folly, if not of treachery, by all? Those who have the most zeal and courage, have little enough to serve their turn for the service that God requires of them: and must this be spent in unworthy babblings, wranglings, and quarrellings? That man's body is in an ill condition that has a sore to which the humours have recourse to feed it, leaving the supply of the parts of the body that are to be nourished and maintained by them: the sore is fed, but the other parts grow lank and feeble. Thus it is with many men's spirits; they are distempered: and then what abilities they have, are drawn away to feed those distempers. What account can be given to God of such a use of them as this?

They make very much against the cause of Christ now in hand, the great work of reformation. Had we joined hand in hand together, and set ourselves to serve the Lord with one shoulder, what abundance of service might have been done! how high might the honour of Christ been advanced among us before this day! But while one draws one way, another another; one seeks to set up, and another labours to pull down; how can the work go on? You will say, that is true indeed, things would go on apace, if those who differ from others would give up their judgments and practices to them, to believe what they believe, and to do what they do. But how can this be? You would not have them give up their judgments or practices to them, till they know them to be right; and how can that be, until they, by discussing, praying, reading, and meditating, find that out? I answer, If some men had certainly found out the right, and other men knew certainly that they had done so, then the work were at an end.

These our dissentions are against a great part of the covenant of grace which God hath made with his people in Christ, and those many promises of so much peace that there is to be in the times of the gospel. We by these do that which tends to make void the covenant; we do, as it were, say Christ is not come in the flesh. 1 John iv, 3: "Every spirit that confesseth not that Christ is come in the flesh, is not of God; and this is that spirit of antichrist." Many men talk much of antichrist; but such as profess the gospel, and yet are of unpeaceable, snarling, contending spirits, they have the spirit of antichrist; and they do not confess that Jesus Christ is come in the flesh. It is an argument the Jews have against Christ; say they, If he were come, then that prophecy, Isaiah xi, 6, would be fulfilled: "The wolf shall dwell with the lamb, and the leopard shall lie down with the kid, and the cow and the bear shall feed together," &c. But this is not so. They also bring many other places where peace is prophesied of, as Isaiah ix, 7: "Of the increase of his government and peace shall be no end." Those who seek for this government, should seek for his peace also.

By our divisions we cross that end that God aimed at, in the variety of his administrations in the gifts and graces of men. That this was not Christ's end in dispensing gifts and graces in a different way, that there might be fuel administered to contentions and quarrels, but rather to exercise love, we spake to before.

Part III
The Cures of Divisions.

WHAT GRACIOUS HEART IS not cut asunder with grief for those sore and fearful evils that there are in, and come from, our divisions; and is not even the second time cut asunder with careful thoughts in itself what may be done to heal them?

Matt. vi, 25, Christ forbids that carking care that cuts our hearts, when it is in matters concerning ourselves, yea, for our lives. "Take no thought for your life;" so it is in your books: but the word signifies, Do not take such thought as should cut your hearts asunder: so v, 28. Why do you divide your hearts? But though this charge of Christ be doubled and doubled again, against our careful, dividing, cutting thoughts about ourselves; yet for the uniting the hearts of the saints together, for the good of the church, this heart-cutting care is not only allowed, but required. 1 Cor. xii, 25: "That there should be no schism in the body; but that the members should have the same care one for another." The words are, "That the members may care the same thing one for another;" and that with dividing, cutting care, that there might be no schism in the body. The word that is here for *care,* is the same that in the former places in the sixth of Matthew is forbidden.

The expressions of my thoughtful cares about this work are the subject of this time. When I set myself about it, my heart doth even ache within me, at the apprehension of the difficulty of it. There are some diseases that are called *opprobria medicorum*, the disgraces of physicians; because they know not what to say or do to them: or if they do anything, it is to little purpose. If there be any soul disease that is *opprobrium theologorum*, the disgrace of divines, it is this of contention and division. How little has all that they have studied, and endeavoured to do, prevailed with the hearts of men! What shall we do? Shall we but join in this one thing, to sit down together, and mourn one over another, till we have dissolved our hearts into tears, and see if we can thus get them to run one into another? O that it might be, what sorrow soever it costs us!

We read (Judges ii, 1-5) that the Lord sent an angel from Gilgal to the men of Israel, who told them how graciously he had dealt with them; yet they had, contrary to the command of God, made a league with the inhabitants of the land, for which the Lord threatened they should be as thorns in their sides. When the angel spake these words to the children of Israel, the people lift up their voice and wept. And they called the name of that place, Bochim, a place of tears. Their sin was too much joining, joining in league where God would not have them: those whom they joined with, God told them should be thorns in their sides. Upon this they wept, and that so sore that the place received its name from their weeping. But O that the Lord would send his angel, yea, his Spirit, to us, to convince us of our evil, that we to this day have not joined in sure league one with another; but are thorns in the sides of one another; and that after so many mercies: yea, that we are so false one to another, though the Lord hath never broke covenant with us, which was the heart-breaking argument the angel used, ver. 1. Yea, the Lord hath done abundantly for us beyond our hopes, desires, and thoughts; and that after all this there should be nothing but breaches and divisions among us; that we should be not only thorns, but spears and swords, in one another's sides, piercing to one another's heart! Are we the children of Israel? Let our hearts then break, and melt, and mourn, and bleed, and resolve that nothing shall comfort them, but peace with our God, and peace one with another.

That one text, 1 Thessalonians iv, 9, were enough alone to pierce our hearts through and through: "As touching brotherly love, ye need not that I write unto you," saith the apostle; "for ye yourselves are taught of God to love one another." O Lord, what, are we in these days such kind of Christians as those were? O that it were so with us, that we had no need to be wrote to, to be preached to, concerning this. Does it appear by our carriage one toward another that we are taught of God to love one another? But that God may teach us this day, attend to what shall be said to you in his name, which I shall cast into *joining principles, considerations, and directions.*

I shall not need to be long in these: for take away dividing principles, dividing distempers, dividing practices, and be thoroughly convinced of the evil of divisions, and one would think our hearts should of themselves run into one another. But that I may not seem to leave our wounds open, so that air should get into them; but endeavour the closing of them, and so the healing; I shall speak something to these heads.

1.
Joining Principles.

The First Joining Principle.

*In the midst of all differences of judgment, and weak-
nesses of the saints, it is not impossible but that they
may live in peace and love together.*

IF, NOTWITHSTANDING THE DIFFERENCES from God's mind,
and many weaknesses, there may be peace and love
between God and his saints: then surely, notwithstanding these things, the saints may be at love and
peace among themselves. Let this be laid for a
ground, and let our hearts be much possessed with
it; we shall find it very helpful to our closing. Away
with that vain conceit which hath been the great
disturber of churches in all ages. If men differ in
their judgment and practice in matters of religion,
though it be in things that are but the weakness of
godly men, yet there must needs be heart-burning
and division. Let all peaceable men deny this consequence: let us not say, it will be so; and that our
words may be made good, afterward indeed make

it so. Certainly the connexion of them, if there be any, is rather from the corruption of our hearts, than from the nature of the things.

"There hath been much ado to get us to agree. We laboured to get our opinions into one, but they will not come together." It may be in our endeavours for agreement we have begun at the wrong end. Let us try what we can do at the other end: it may be we shall have better success there. Let us labour to join our hearts, to engage our affections one to another. If we cannot be of one mind that we may agree, let us agree that we may be of one mind.

The Second Joining Principle.

That shall never be got by strife that may be had by love and peace.

We would all fain have our wills. Now that which lies uppermost upon many men's heart's [*sic*]; that which is the first thing they do, if their wills be crossed, is presently to strive and contend: but this should be the last thing, after all other means are tried; and should never be made use of but in case of pure necessity. We should first think, Is there any way in the world whereby it is possible we may have our desires satisfied with peace? Let us try this, and another way, a third, a fourth, yea, a hundred ways, if they lie between us and the way of strife, before we come to meddle with that.

Among those means, he directs for union when St. Paul speaks of love: "I will show you," says he, "a more excellent way;" a way of the highest excellency, beyond any expression. The way of love, of engaging hearts one to another, is the only way to bring persons into unity of judgment; yea, the only way, when all is done, for men to have their wills. I may give you this or the other rule, to bring you to think and do the same thing; but that which hath an excellency in it with an hyperbole, is the way of love. If you could get your minds to agree by other ways, certainly you could not enjoy it with that sweetness and comfort, as you may if you get it this way. Certainly there is no man living but hath cause to repent him that ever he got that by strife and contention that he might have got by love and peace. What hinders why soft and gentle words may not prevail, as well as hard and bitter language? Why may not a loving, winning carriage, do as much as severe, rigid violence? If it may, thou providest ill for thine own peace and comfort, to leave this way and betake thyself to the other. Tell me, were it a sign of valour in a man to draw his sword at every insect that comes near him? yea, at every fly that lights upon him? Were it not folly and madness? Why, he may by putting forth his finger put them off from him. Thy froward, choleric spirit, is ready to draw at everything that thou likest not. This is thy folly; for thou mayest, with less ado, have what thou hast a mind to. If I would put a feather from me, I need not strike violently at it. A soft, gentle breath, will do it better. Why should a man labour and toil till he sweats again, to take up a pin? Have none of you sometimes made a great stir in your families about that which, when the stir is a little over, you plainly see you might have done as well with a word speaking? None but a cruel, harsh, sordid-spirited man, will say, I had rather men should fear me than love me. God prizes most what he hath from us by love.

The Third Joining Principle.

It is letter to do good than to receive good.

Active good is better than passive. Only God himself, his angels, and saints, do good; but all creatures can receive good. This principle would quickly join us; for if this were in men's hearts, they would study to do all the good they could to one another, and to gain upon one another's hearts; and the more good we do to any, the more will our hearts be inclinable to love them. The very communication of goodness, if it be out of a good spirit, carries the heart along with it to the subject this good is communicated to. The more good God doth to any, the more he loves them. So it is with us in our proportion. If you take a poor child from the dunghill, or out of the alms-house, and make him your heir, you do not only this good to him because you love him, but you love more because you look upon him as an object of your goodness — as one raised by you.

The Fourth Joining Principle.

The good of other men is my good as well as theirs.

We are all of one body. Whatever good others have, it is the good of the body. It makes them some way able to do that good that we should have done, or at least that we should desire to have done.

Community in the church is more. 1 Cor. iii, 22: "Whether Paul, or Apollos, or Cephas, or the world, or life, or death, or things present, or things to come, all are yours; you are Christ's, and Christ is God's." If you be godly, you have an interest in all the eminently godly men in the world: in all their gifts, graces, and in all they have or do. All that is in the world, that hath any good in it, is yours; yea, what is evil shall be serviceable to you for good. This is brought by the apostle to quiet the jarrings and contentions that were among the Corinthians. One would be for Paul, another for Apollos. Says the apostle, What need this contention who you are for, and who another is for? they are all yours. All the excellency there is in them is the good of every one of you. A special reason why men contend so much is, they think the good that other men have is their evil; therefore they must either get it to themselves, or darken it in those that have it. But such men, acted by such a principle, are poor, low-spirited men. A man of a raised, enlarged spirit, opens his heart that it may be filled with that infinite good in which there is all good. Now if it be that good my soul closeth with, and is satisfied in, then whatever hath any goodness in it, be it where it will, it flows from this infinite ocean of good my soul is launched into, and some way or other flows into this again. Though, through men's corruptions, there may be windings and turnings in the course of it, yet hither it comes at last: and, therefore, it is mine as really and truly as any I have in mine own hand. My soul then shall rejoice in all the good I see my brethren have, and in all they do. I will bless God for it, and seek the furtherance of it what I can. Surely this man must needs be a man of peace and love.

The Fifth Joining Principle.

My good is more in the public than in myself.

It is because we have such private spirits, that there are such contentions among us. Were we more public-spirited, our contentions would vanish. When I read of what public spirits many of the heathens were, I am ashamed to look upon many Christians. Paulus Æmilius, hearing of the death of his children, spake with an undaunted courage thus: "That the gods had heard his prayer, which was, that calamities should rather befall his family than the commonwealth." The publicness of his spirit made it very sweet and lovely. The story says of him, he entreated them gently and graciously whom he had subdued, setting forward their causes, even as if they had been his confederates, very friends, and near kinsmen. Public-spirited men are men of sweet and peaceable spirits.

The Sixth Joining Principle.

*What I would have others do to me, that will I
endeavour to do to them.*

Would not I have others bear with me? I then will bear
with them. I would have others do offices of kindness to
me; I will then do offices of kindness to them. I would
have the carriage of others lovely, and amiable to me;
mine shall be so to them. I would have others live peaceably with me; I will do so with them. This rule of doing to
others as I would be done to, is a law of justice; such justice as keeps the peace.

Chrysostom, in his thirteenth sermon to the people of
Antioch, makes use of this principle. Thus after Christ
had spoken of many blessednesses, says he, "Those things
you would have others to do to you, do you to them. As if
he should say, 'There needs not many words; let thine
own will be thy law. Would you receive benefits? bestow
benefits then. Would you have mercy? be merciful then.
Would you be loved? then love. Be you the judge yourself, be you the lawgiver of your own life. That which
you hate, do not to another. Cannot you endure reproach?
do not you reproach others. Cannot you endure to have
others envy you? do not you envy others. Cannot you
endure to be deceived? do not you deceive others.'"

The Seventh Joining Principle.

*It is as great an honour to have my will by yielding,
as by overcoming.*

Many men in their anger will say, I will be even with
him. I will tell you a way how you may be above him:
forgive him. By yielding, pardoning, putting up the
wrong, you show you have power over yourself, and
this is a greater thing than to have power over another.

Numb. xiv, 17: "Now, I beseech thee, let the power of my Lord be great." "Pardon, I beseech thee, the iniquity of this people." Verse 19. By this thou mayest honourably prevail with thy brother. Hereby shalt thou heap coals of fire upon his head.

If a man offend me merely through weakness, this is his affliction. In this he is neither an enemy to himself nor me. He mourns for it, and I will pity him in his mourning. He is more troubled for what he hath done, than I have cause to be for what I have suffered. If he offend willingly and purposely, he is his own enemy more than mine. When Latimer was cozened in buying a commodity, his friends telling him how he was cheated of his money, he fell to mourning for him that had cheated him. "He hath the worst of it," said he. If my heart rise against a man in this, and I seek to oppose him in his way, it may very well be interpreted to be out of love to him; for my heart rises against his enemy. I oppose his enemy, even himself; but an enemy to himself more than to me. He hath hurt me a little, but himself more. I am troubled a little for the wrong I suffer, but more for the evil he hath done. If his ways be enmity to God, I will oppose him, because I love God, and no further than wherein I may manifest my love to God, rather than hatred of him. When Servetus condemned Zuinglius for his harshness, he answered, "In other things I will be mild, but not so in blasphemies against God." Let us keep our enmity within these bounds, and the peace of God will not be broke.

If, when others wrong you, you care not what you do to right yourself, this is your folly and madness. Such a one hurt me, and I will therefore mischief myself: he hath pricked me with a pin, and I will therefore in anger run my knife into my side. If in all we suffer, we be sure to keep from righting ourselves by any ways of sin, there will not be much peace broke. Such a one is thine enemy; and wilt thou of one enemy make two? Wilt thou also be an enemy to thyself? Yea, a greater enemy than he or any man living can be to thee? For all the men in the world cannot make thee sin, except thou wilt thyself.

A father hath not so much power over his child, as to provoke him. Col. iii, 21: "Fathers, provoke not your children to wrath." Surely if a man hath not this power over his child, he hath it not over his friend, his neighbour, much less his superior. Yet how many take delight in this, "Such a thing I know will anger him, and he shall be sure to have it!" O wicked heart! dost thou see that this will be a temptation to thy brother, and wilt thou lay it before him? Dost thou not pray for thyself and for him, "Lord, lead us not into temptation?" "We should account it the greatest evil to us of all the evil of afflictions, to be any occasion of sin to our brother; but what an evil should this be to us, to provoke our brother to sin? If we will needs be provoking, then let the apostle's exhortation prevail with us, Heb. x, 24: "Let us consider one another to provoke unto love and good works." Let us not consider one another in a way of curiosity and emulation, to envy, or find fault with one another, from whence frowardness, pride, hatred, dissentions, factions, may arise, saith Hyperius upon the place; but consider one another, so as we may further the good of one another, so as to make one another quick and active in that which is good.

But how will this join us one to another?

Answ. Very much; both as it holds forth the goodness of peace with all men, and as it carries the heart strongly to the making and keeping peace with God and a man's own conscience. This peace with God and a man's own conscience will so sweeten the heart, that it cannot but be sweet toward every one. A man who hath satisfaction enough within, can easily bear affliction and troubles that come without. When Saul had made great breaches between God and his soul, and in his own conscience, then he grew to be of a very froward spirit toward every man.

Before his apostasy he was of a very meek and quiet spirit, but this soured his spirit, and made it grow harsh, rugged, and cruel. This is the cause of the frowardness of many men and women in their families, and with their neighbours; there are secret breaches between God and their own consciences.

2.
Considerations.

GOD IS LOVE. THERE is anger and hatred in God as well as love: but God is never said to be anger or hatred; no, not justice itself: but he loves that expression of himself to the children of men, *God is love*. If God intended that all things among men, either in church or commonwealth, should be carried with strictness of justice, he would rather have governed his church and the world by angels— who have right apprehensions of justice, who are themselves perfect, altogether free from those evils that are to be punished— than by men, whose apprehensions of justice are exceeding weak, unconstant, partial, as often false as true, and have much of that in themselves, that they judge in others.

"When our yielding is through ignorance, cowardice, base fear, and not from a principle of wisdom and understanding; it is not so much out of true love to peace, as a foolish, ignorant, sottish, sordid spirit, of our own: whereas had we had a spirit of wisdom and courage, we might have peace upon more honourable terms. Indeed, many think every kind of yielding baseness; but they are, for the most part, such as are not put to any great trial themselves. But when our conscience tells us, that what we do is what the rule allows us, it is not because we would avoid trouble, but we find, through God's grace, our hearts in some measure prepared for suffering, if God were pleased to call us to it, in anything wherein he may have glory, and the public may be benefited; but because, all things duly considered, we see that God in such a way shall have more glory, and our brethren generally more good. Therefore, whatever becomes of our particular satisfaction in regard of esteem, or otherwise, we are willing to yield; because in this we find our hearts as much closing with God, enjoying communion with him in all holiness and godly fear; and in other things that go as near to us, we are able to deny ourselves as much as ever. In this we may have comfort, that it is not baseness that makes us yield, but rather the grace of God enabling us to rule over our own spirits. The peace that we thus purchase with the suffering much in our names, and the loss of many comforts, does not cost us too dear.

God hath joined us together as we are men. We are not dogs, not wolves. Then let us not be so to one another. Acts vii, 26, Moses speaks thus to those who strove one with another: "Sirs, ye are brethren; why do you wrong one another?" There is a consideration in this, that ye are *men*. If there were no more, ye should not strive one with another: but much more considering ye are *brethren*. If we be men, let us be humane. What is the meaning of humanity, but courteousness, gentleness, and pleasantness, in our carriage one to another? But still the consideration grows higher, as we are the same countrymen, of old acquaintance, in the same employment, of the same family and kindred; but, above all, joined in such a blessed root, the fountain of all love and peace. Ephes. iv, 4, presents this consideration most fully to us. The reason the apostle gives why we must keep the unity of the Spirit in the bond of peace, is, because "there is one body, and one Spirit; ye are called in one hope; one Lord, one faith, one baptism, one God and Father of all." Here you have seven ones together in two or three lines. It is very much that the Spirit of God should join so close together seven ones. Surely it is to be a strong argument for us to unity.

1. One body: the meanest member is in the body. Is it comely for the body of Christ to be rent and torn? Any reference to Christ might persuade unity; but union with Christ as the members with the body, what heart can stand against the strength of this? What can cause one member to tear and rend another, but madness?

2. One spirit: 1 Cor. xii, 11, "that one and the self-same spirit." He does not only say, the *same spirit*, but *the self-same spirit*; and, as if that was not enough, he adds *one* to the *self-same*; and that yet not enough, he says *that one*. The repeating the article hath a great elegancy in it. And is not this one spirit of love and meekness? What does a froward, contentious spirit, do in thee, who professest thyself to be a Christian? What, says Cyprian, does the fierceness of wolves, the madness of dogs, the deadly poison of serpents, the bloody rage of beasts, in a Christian's breast?

3. Called in one hope, are you not heirs, joint heirs, of the same kingdom? And do you contend as if one belonged to the kingdom of light, and the other to the kingdom of darkness?

4. One Lord. You serve the same Lord and Master. Is it for the credit of a master, that his servants are always wrangling and fighting one with another? Is it not a tedious thing in a family that the servants can never agree? Mark how ill the Lord takes this. Matt. xxiv, 49-51. That evil servant who begins to smite his fellow-servants, provokes his Lord against him, so as to come upon him with such severity as to cut him asunder, and to appoint his portion with the hypocrites; or, as it is in the Greek, he

will divide him in two. He by his smiting his fellow-servants makes divisions, but his Lord will divide him. It may be he pretends that his fellow-servants do not do their duty as they ought, as if he were more careful of the honour of his Lord than others. But in the mean while he inveighs against others, smiting them with the tongue, and otherwise, as he is able. He sits at full tables, eats and drinks of the best, with such as are carnal and sensual. But they are great men; to have their countenance is brave. This is extremely suitable to a carnal heart, who yet keeps up a profession of religion, and hath some form of godliness. He is afraid to lose his fleshly contentment, therefore he smites those who stand in his way. Thus divisions and troubles are made in God's family. The Lord, the Master of it, will reward accordingly. He will divide such, by cutting them asunder, and appointing their portion with the hypocrites.

5. One faith. What though we agree not together in some things of lesser moment, yet we agree in one faith. Why should we not then keep the unity of the Spirit in the bond of peace? The agreement in the faith one would think should swallow up all the disagreements. We should rather bless God for keeping men sound in the faith, than contend with them for lesser mistakes. When the Pharisees (Acts xxiii, 9) understood that Paul agreed with them in that great doctrine of the resurrection, they presently overlooked his other differences, saying, "We find no evil in this man." Our brethren agree with us in more fundamentals than this, and yet we can find evil in them, and aggravate their evil beyond what it is, and improve it all we can against them. This is worse than Pharisaical.

Mr. Calvin, writing to our countrymen at Frankford, (who fled for their lives in witness to the truth, yet miserably jarring and contending one against another there, to the scandal of all the churches of God in those parts) begins his epistle thus: "This doth grievously torment: it is extremely absurd that dissensions should arise among brethren, exiles, fled from their country for the same faith, and for that cause which alone in this your scattering, ought to be to you as a holy band, to keep you fast bound together." Their contentions were about church worship.

6. One baptism. We are baptized into Christ's death. And is not that to show that we should be dead to all those things in the world that cause strife and contention among men? Our baptism is our badge, our livery. It furthers somewhat the unity of servants that they wear all one livery.

7. One God. Though there be three persons in the divine nature, and every person is God, yet there is but one God. Here is a union infinitely beyond all unions that any creature can be capable of. The mystery of this union is revealed to us, to make us in love with union. Our interest in this one God is such a conjunction, as nothing can be more.

Joseph's brethren (Gen. 1, 17) looked upon this as having very great power in it to make up all breaches, to heal old grudges. After their father was dead, their consciences misgave them for what they had done to Joseph. They were afraid old matters would break forth, and that Joseph would turn their enemy. Now how do they seek to unite Joseph's heart to them? "We pray thee," say they, "forgive the trespass of the servants of the God of thy father." And the text says, "Joseph wept when they spake unto him." O this was a heart-breaking speech to Joseph! The servants of the God of my father! Shall my heart ever be estranged from the servants of the God of my father? The Lord forbid! This offence indeed was great; but their God is my God, and he was my father's God! This argument had more in it to draw Joseph's heart to them, than if they had said we are your brethren, we come from the loins you did. True that is something, but the servants of the God of thy father is much more. Let us look upon all the godly, though they have many weaknesses, and have not carried themselves toward us as they ought; yet they are the servants, yea, the children of our God, and of our father's God. Let this draw our hearts to them. If they be one with us in their interest in one God, let them be one with us in heart affection, to love, delight, and rejoice in communion with them.

One God and Father. Mal. ii, 10; Job xxxi, 15. Is it seemly that one man's children should be always contending, quarrelling and villifying [*sic*] one another? Do you think this is pleasing to your Father, who is above all and through all? You have enough in your Father to satisfy your souls for ever. Whatever you want other ways, he hath put honour enough upon you that he is your Father. Why will ye contend and quarrel about trifles? "He worketh in all, and is in all." This scripture is one of the most famous for the union of the saints in one, that we have in all the book of God. You will say, If we could see God in such, if we could see grace and holiness in them, our hearts would unite; but we see not these. Answer. Take heed thou dost not reject any from being thy brother, whom Jesus Christ at the great day will own for his, and God the Father will call his child. Many men are of such spirits, they love to be altogether busied about their brethren's differences. It is upon these their tongues and pens run; not to heal, but widen them. You shall not hear them speak about their agreements; their strength is not bent to strengthen them. Or, if at any time they do take notice of their union, it is to make them more odious: or to strengthen themselves in what they differ from them. They desire to get in men, and to get from them, only to serve their own turns. This is an evil spirit.

Let us consider men's tempers, spirits, temptations, age, gifts. There must be a due consideration of all these, and we must indulge something to them all. This would allay much strife, as we read Num. xxxi, 21. We must deal with every man according to his temper. Some men are by their complexions of a more harsh and rugged temper than others. Consider what is the best way of dealing with such. In the main they are faithful and useful, will join with and spend their lives for you. If the harshness of their natures cause excrescences, unpleasing carriages; consider their tempers. Though no evil in them is to be justified, yet deal tenderly with them, indulge them what lawfully you may.

Some men's spirits, though upright to God and you, have a fervour in them that is not qualified with that degree of wisdom, meekness, and humility, as they ought. Do not presently take those advantages against them, which they may perhaps give you. Do not fly upon them as if those unjustifiable expressions that drop from them, come from a malignant spirit. You know the men, and the manner of their communication. Then pass by weaknesses.

Some men's temptations are very strong. It may be their hearts are pressed with disappointments; they may be pierced with the wants of many comforts you enjoy; they have family and personal temptations that you are freed from: you do not know what you might do under the like temptations.

Bless God that you are delivered from them. Do not add to your brethren's affliction by taking advantage against them; but, according to the rule of the apostle, Gal. vi, 1, consider, some all their days have lived in wicked families, disorderly communities, and never were acquainted with the society of the saints, and that way of godliness that hath the most strictness and power in it.

You must not deal with them the same way you would deal with others, who have a godly education, and early and long acquaintance with the most strict and powerful ways of godliness, but now oppose them. Consider men's years. Old age looks for respect, and justly too; especially such as have gone through the brunt, and suffered much for your good. Though some infirmities should break forth, that are incident to old age, we must cover and pass by what we can, not forgetting that respect is due to the hoary head found in the way of righteousness. Consider men's gifts, that may be they are not able to understand what you do. Thank God for your strength, but be not angry with your brother because he is weaker.

What we get by contention will never quit cost. If thou hast so much command of thy spirit, canst so far overcome thy passions, as to get time in cool blood to cast up thy accounts truly, what good thou hast done, or what thou hast got by such contentions; and on the other side, cast up what hurt thou hast done, what sin hath been committed by thee and thy party, what evil hath got into thy spirit; I fear you will have little cause to boast of, or rejoice in, your gains.

To be freed from that expense that comes in by strife, is not a little gain, says Ambrose. In strife you will find there is a very great expense of time, gifts, and learning. Many men, with the good gifts God hath given them, might have proved shining lights in the church; but, by reason of their contentious spirits, prove no other than smoking firebrands. It may be, by all the stir you keep, you will never get your end; if you do, it will not quit cost; the charge you have been at, comes to more than it is worth. God deliver me from having my end at such a dear rate!

The strongest have need of the weakest; therefore, let not the hand say it hath no need of the foot, nor the eye that it hath no need of the hand. God hath so tempered the body, that every member hath need of every member. Little nails may be useful where great wedges can do no good: little chips may help to set great logs on fire.

Consider, when men provoke us we are ready to fly

upon them, looking no further than the men with whom we are displeased. But take another sight, and perhaps you may see the devil on the other side the hedge, who hath been the chief agent in this business. He prepares his net, Augustine saith, to catch men in: he raises up contentions, and causes much trouble to be in churches and among brethren. You think all the evil is in the trouble of your contentions. O no; the devil is behind: he intends to bring some of you into some great sin by these things. He hath set his net for you. When you are troubled and vexed by such contentions, the devil sees you fit for a temptation. Now I hope, says he, to get him to do such things, which otherwise I could never have got him to. O that we had hearts, when we find contention stirring, to consider, but is there not a temptation and ruin in them?

Consider how the heart of God is set upon making peace with us. He was in Christ reconciling the world to himself. This work hath taken up the thoughts, council, and heart of God, above anything that he ever did. This is the chief master-piece of all his works. There is more of the glory of God in this than in all that he hath done. This is, and shall be, the grand subject of admiration for saints and angels; the matter of their praises to all eternity. God was resolved to have it whatever it cost him, though the price were more than ten thousand worlds were worth. It was no less than the blood of the Son of God, the second person in the Trinity, God blessed for evermore. Col. i, 14. What God hath done for peace with us, calls aloud to us to prize peace one with another. It is the apostle's sentiments. 1 John iii, 16. If it cost Christ his life to make our peace with God, we should be willing to do anything we are able, even to the hazard of our lives, to make peace among the saints. Christ laid down his life for this peace. Also (Eph. ii, 14) Christ reconciles both unto God. But how? It is in one body. Lay this consideration near and warm to your hearts, and it will comfort you, and so preserve and increase peaceable dispositions in you toward one another.

Remember, God hath called us to peace. That case upon which the apostle mentions our calling to peace, is as difficult a case to preserve peace in, as any can fall out in one's life. It was that of being unequally yoked, one a believer, and the other an infidel; yet being man and wife, he determines that the believer must be content to live with the unbeliever, as it becomes a wife or husband, except he or she of themselves will depart; but they should give them no occasion of departing, but by their holy conversation seek to convert them. This was counted a hard task; but it must be, saith the apostle, and grounds it upon this, God hath called us to peace.

There is another case, almost as difficult as the former, where patience and quietness of spirit are put to trial; that is, when a servant meets with a harsh, rugged, cruel master, that treats him wrongfully. One would think this might be allowed to put the spirit into a rage. No, saith the apostle; such must be the command you must have over your spirits, that you must patiently bear this; and he grounds it upon, for hereunto are ye called. 1 Pet. ii, 21, 22. "But though husbands and wives should live at peace; though they suffer one from another; though servants should put up with wrongs from their masters: yet it follows not that the like patience should be required in us when we are wronged by our equals, by those to whom we have no such band of relation to tie us." Yes, the argument is strong in this case also. 1 Pet. iii, 8, 9.

Consider the presence of God and of Christ. Our God, Father, Master, and Saviour, stands by, looking on us. It is a most excellent passage that I find in an epistle of Luther to the ministers of Nuringburg. There were great divisions among them, he wrote to pacify their spirits one toward another. "Suppose," says he, "you saw Jesus

Christ standing before you, and by his very eyes speaking thus unto your hearts, What do you, O my dear children, whom I have redeemed with my blood, begotten again by my Spirit, to that end that you might love one another; know that this is the mark of my disciples. Leave this business, cast it wholly upon me. I will look to it, there is no danger that the church should suffer by this, though it should be stilled; yea, though it should die: but there is a great deal of danger if you dissent among yourselves, if you bite one another. Do not thus sadden my Spirit, do not spoil the angels of their joys in heaven; am not I more to you than all matters between you? than all your afflictions and all your offences? What, can any words of a brother, any unjust trouble, penetrate your hearts, stick so fast in you as my wounds, as my blood, as all that I am to you— your Saviour Jesus Christ?" O that we had such real apprehensions of Christ looking upon, and speaking unto us!

Let every man consider his own weaknesses. You are now ready to take offence from others, and within awhile you are as likely to be as offensive to others. There will then be as much need that they should bear with you, as now there is that you should bear with them. A common law of those who intend to live at peace one with another, is, we desire pardon, and we give pardon.

Now let us consider our mortality. It is but a little time we have to live. Shall the greater part of it, nay, why should any part of it, be spent in contentions and quarrels? Sprinkle upon your hearts the meditations of death, that in a little while this flesh of yours will be turned to dust; let this quiet you.

Consider what account we can give to Jesus Christ, of all our divisions, in the day of judgment.

When Christ shall come, will you stand before him with scratched faces, with black and blue eyes? 1 Thess. iii, 12, 13. It will be a sad thing to be found in our divisions at the coming of Jesus Christ! Matt. xxiv, 50, the coming of Christ is mentioned as a terror to those who shall but begin to smite their fellow-servants.

We may wrangle and stand out one against another in our contentions now, but it will not be so easy to answer Jesus Christ, as it is to answer one to another. In the name of Jesus Christ I now speak unto you; yea, as from him, I beseech and charge you, let no reason move you to contend with, dissent, or separate from, your brethren, but that which you are persuaded in your consciences, and that after deep and serious examination, will hold out before, and will be approved by, Jesus Christ at his coming.

3.
Directions.

FIRST. OBSERVE THIS GENERAL direction. See that you forget not the great difference between novices and experienced Christians: between the babes and those of full age: between the weak and the strong in grace. Level them not in your estimation. It is not for nothing that the Spirit of God in Scripture maketh so great a difference between them, as you may read in Heb. v, 11-14; vi, 1, 2; 1 Tim. iii, 6; 1 John ii, 12-14. There are babes, strong men, and fathers, among Christians. There are some that are dull of hearing, and have need of milk, and are unskilful in the word of righteousness, and must be taught the principles: and there are others who can digest strong meat, who by reason of use, have their senses exercised to discern both good and evil. It is not for nothing that the younger are commanded reverence and submission to the elder, and that the pastors and governors of the church are usually called by the name of elders; because it was supposed that the elder sort were more experienced and wise; and, therefore, pastors and rulers were to be chosen out of them. And why is it that children must so much honour their fathers and mothers, and must be governed by them? It is not merely because generation giveth the parents a propriety in their children; for God would not have folly to be the governor of wisdom, upon pretence of such propriety: but it is also because it must ordinarily be supposed, that infants are ignorant, and parents have understanding, and are fit to be their teachers, as having had longer time and helps to learn, and more experience to make their knowledge clear and firm. If the young and unexperienced were ordinarily as wise as the aged or mature, why are not children made governors of their parents, or at least commanded to instruct and teach them, as ordinarily as parents must do their children? The Lord Jesus himself would be subject to his mother and reputed father in his childhood. Luke ii, 51. Can there be a livelier conviction of the arrogance of those novices, who proudly slight the judgments of their elders, as presuming, groundlessly, that they are wiser than they? Yea, Christ would not enter upon his public ministry or office, till he was about thirty years of age. Luke iii, 23. He is blind that perceiveth not, in this example, a most notorious condemnation of the pride of those that hasten to be teachers of others before they have had time or means to learn; and that deride or vilify the judgments of the aged, who differ from their conceits, before they understand the things in which they are so confident. It was thought a good answer in John ix, 21: "He is of age; ask him." But they that are under age now think their words to be the wisest, because they are the boldest and fiercest. The old were wont to bless the young, and now the young deride the old. It is the character of a turbulent people, (Deut. xxviii, 50,) that they regard not the person of the aged; that is, they reverence not their age. How many vehement commands are there in Solomon's proverbs to the younger sort, to hearken to the counsel of their parents. The contrary was the ruin of Eli's sons, and the shame of Samuel's. 1 Sam. viii, 1, 5. Was Rehoboam unwise in forsaking the counsel of the aged, and hearkening to the young and rash? and are those people wise that, in the mysteries of salvation, will prefer the vehement passions of a novice before the well-settled judgment of the experienced, aged ministers? I know that the old are too often ignorant, and that wisdom doth not always increase with our ages; but I know withal that children are never fit to be the rulers of the church; and that old men may be foolish, but young men are never wise enough for so high a work. We are not now considering what may fall out rarely as a wonder, but what is ordinarily to be expected. Most of the church's confusions and divisions have been caused by the younger sort of Christians, who are in the heat of their zeal, and the infancy of understanding; who have affection enough to make them drive on, but have not judgment enough to know the way. None are so fierce and rash in condemning the things and persons which they understand not, and in raising clamours against all that are wiser and soberer than they. If they once take a thing to be a sin, which is no sin, or a duty which is no duty, there is no person, no minister, no magistrate, who hath age, or wisdom, or piety enough, to save them from the injuries of juvenile temerity, if they do not think and speak, and do according to their green and raw conceits. Remember, therefore, to be always sensible of the great disadvantages of youth, and to preserve that reverence for experienced age, which God in nature as well as in Scripture hath made their due. If time and labour were not necessary to maturity of knowledge, why do you not trust another with your health, as well as an experienced physician; and with your estates, as well as a studied lawyer? And why do not seamen trust any other to govern the ship, as well as an experienced pilot? Do you not see that all men ordinarily are best at that which, by long study, they have made their profession? I know those that I have now to do with, will say, that "divinity is not learned by labour and men's teaching, as other sciences and arts are; but by the teaching of the Spirit of God; and, therefore, the youngest may have as much of it as the eldest.["]

Answ. There is some truth and some falsehood, and much confusion, in this objection. It is true that the saving knowledge of divinity must be taught by the Spirit of God: and it is false that labour and human teaching are not the means which must be used by them who will have the teaching of the Spirit.

1. Consider, I pray, why else it is, God hath so multiplied commands to dig for it as for silver, and search for it as a hidden treasure; to cry for knowledge, and lift up our voice for understanding; to wait at the posts of wisdom's doors; to search the Scriptures, and meditate on them day and night. Is not this such study and labour as men use to get understanding in other professions? Are not these the plain commands of God? And are they not then deceivers who contradict them?

2. Is it not blaspheming of God's Spirit to make it the patron of men's sloth and idleness, under pretence of magnifying grace, when so many texts command

diligence, and slothfulness is so great a sin? And none are so forward to preach as these same men that cry down men's teaching.

3. Why hath God settled a teaching office in his church, and commanded all to attend, and hear and learn, if we are taught by the Spirit without man's help? Why were the apostles sent out into all the world? And why were they commanded to teach all nations, and to teach the church all that Christ commanded them? And why doth he promise to be with them to the end of the world? But that this is the way of the Spirit's teaching, to teach those first who are our outward teachers, and then to help us to understand them. And those are taught of God, who are taught by those who are sent of God to be their teachers, and have the inward concurrence of his grace. Therefore remember to give due respect to them who have been longer in Christ than you, and to them who have longer studied the Scriptures, and to them that have had greater helps and experience; and do not too easily imagine, that those who are below them in all these advantages, are yet above them in sound understanding: though such a wonder may sometimes come to pass.

Direction II.

Observe well the secret and subtle workings of spiritual pride, and how deep-rooted and dangerous a sin it is, and what special temptations to this odious sin the younger and empty-headed Christians have; that the resistance of them may be your daily care.

Pride is the self-idolizing sin; the great rebel against God; the chief part of the devil's image; that one sin which breaketh every commandment; the heart of the old man; the root and parent, and summary, of all other sin; the antichristian vice which is most directly contrary to the life of Christ; the principal object of God's hatred and disdain, and the mark of those whom he delighteth to tread down; and the certain prognostic of dejection and abasement, either by humbling repentance or damnation. It is called *spiritual pride* from the object; when men are proud of spiritual excellencies, real or supposed. And this is so much worse than pride in beauty, apparel, riches, high places, or high birth, as the abuse of great and excellent things is worse than the abuse of vanities and trifles; and as things spiritual are in themselves more contrary to the nature of pride, and therefore the sin hath the greater enormity. The common exercise of this religious or spiritual pride is first about knowledge, and secondly about our godliness or goodness. 1st. Pride of our understandings worketh thus: first, a man that was formerly in darkness, is much affected with the new-come light, and perceiveth that he knoweth much more than he did before; and then groweth to a carnal and corrupt estimation of it, valuing it more as nature is pleased with it, than as it is sanctified by it: delighting in knowledge for itself, more than for the purity, love, and heavenliness, which it should effect. Then he looketh about him on the ignorant sort of people, who know not what he knoweth, and seeth how far they are below him; and he thinketh within himself, What a difference hath God made between me and them. And because thankfulness is a duty, he observeth not how pride doth twist itself with it, and creeps in under the protection of its name. And how thankfulness and pride have the same expressions, and both of them say, "I thank thee, O Father, that thou hast hid these things from the wise and prudent, and hast revealed them to babes." "I thank thee, God, that I am not as other men are, extortioners, unjust, adulterers, or even as this publican." Luke xviii, 11. And then he is so taken up with the things which he knoweth, that he perceiveth not what knowledge he yet wanteth. And the deep affection which his knowledge worketh in him, or the tickling pleasure which he hath in knowing, joined with this ignorance of his in other things, doth make him over confident of all his apprehensions, as if everything which he imagineth were an absolute certainty: and so he wanteth that humble suspicion of his own understanding, which a true acquaintance with his ignorance would have caused in him. And thus he groweth to overvalue all his own conceivings, and to undervalue all the opinions and reasonings of others which are contrary to his own. And thence he proceeds to corrupt his religion with such misapprehensions, rejects divine institutions, and sanctifies human traditions as divine dictates; and having made him a religion of his own, he confidently thinketh that it is of God. And next he valueth all men that he hath to do with, according as they are nearer or farther off from this which he accounteth the way of God. He chooseth whom he will join with by the test of this religion, which his pride hath chosen. He zealously declaimeth against the opposers of this way, as against the adversaries of truth and godliness, and consequently of God himself. He prayeth up his opinions, and preacheth them up, and contendeth for them; and prayeth, and preacheth, and disputeth down, all that is against them. He laboureth to strengthen the party that is for them, and to weaken that which is against them. And thus he divideth the kingdom and family of Christ: he destroyeth first the love of his brother and neighbour in himself, and then laboureth to destroy it in all others, by speaking against those that are not of his mind with contempt and obloquy, to represent them as an unlovely sort of men; and if the interest of his cause do require it, perhaps he will next destroy their persons. And yet all this is done in zeal for God, and as an acceptable service to him; and they think all are neuters and lukewarm, who prosecute not the schism so fervently as they, and fight not against love with as much vehemency: yea, and in all this they are still confident that they love the brethren with a special love, and make it the mark that they are Christ's disciples, and that they are passed from death to life, because they love the persons who are of their own opinion and way, and because they love their own image, which is only self-love reflected.

And thus *Pride* insensibly, while they perceive it not at all, doth choose their opinions, their religions, their parties, and make their duties and their sins, and rule their judgments, affections, and actions; which is all but the same thing which the Scripture in one word calleth *heresy*. And all that I have said, you may find said in other words in the third chapter of James. And there are two things which greatly promote this sin: the one is conceit that all their apprehensions are the Spirit's dictates, or the effect of its illumination; and the works and teachings of the Spirit are not to be contradicted, or suspected, but to be honoured. Therefore they think it is a resisting of the Spirit, to resist their judgment. And they are persuaded that their apprehensions are caused by the Spirit, partly because they had no such thing while they lived in wickedness, but it came in either with their change, or shortly after, and therefore they think that the same light which showed them their sinful state, doth show them also all these principles; and partly because they find themselves as deeply affected with these misapprehensions, as with others which are sound and right: therefore they are confident that they come from the same Spirit. And especially when these thoughts come in upon the reading of the Scripture, or in meditation, or after earnest prayer to God to teach them by his Spirit, and lead them into the truth, and not to suffer them to err; and when they find they have good ends and meanings, and a desire to know the truth; all this persuadeth them that it is the Spirit from whom their thoughts proceed, when yet it may be no such thing.

And another much greater, and more common cause

of this self-conceitedness, is this: all men's understandings are naturally imperfect. Our knowledge about natural things is small and dark, much more about supernatural: the wisest must say, *We know but in part.* And the variety of men's degrees of knowledge, joined with the difference of their education, and advantages, and foregoing thoughts, do make as great a diversity of understandings, as of complexions; and yet it is very hard to any man to have a sufficient diffidence and suspicion of his mistaken mind. For what a man knoweth, he knoweth that he knoweth. But no man that erreth, doth know that he erreth, for that is a contradiction.

And there is a religious pride of goodness, as well as of knowledge, which must yet more carefully be avoided, as being yet worse than the former, as the thing abused is much better. And this worketh as secretly and as subtly as the former. It may not only consist with many complaints, and confessions of sinfulness, weakness, and unworthiness, but even with doubts of sincerity, and so much dejectedness as seemeth to draw near to desperation. It is an ordinary thing to hear the same persons talking in a complaining, doubting, and almost despairing manner of speech, and yet to have high expectations of respect from others, and to be most proudly impatient of the least undervaluing or neglect. Yea, pride will make an advantage to itself of all those humble confessions and complaints: and it is an old observation, that many are proud of their humility. For though it be true, as Austin saith, that grace is a thing that no man can use amiss; the meaning is only that grace efficiently can do nothing amiss, (for if it do amiss, so far it is not grace;) yet objectly all grace may be abused, that is, a man may make it the object of his pride, and the occasion of many other sins. And this religious pride of goodness doth ordinarily work under the pretext of thankfulness to God for his grace, and zeal for holiness; but it may be known by this, that it always tendeth to lift us up, and to the diminishing of love to others, and the contempt of the weak, and the censuring of our brethren, and the divisions and disturbance of the church of God. They are lamentable effects which this pride produceth in the church, and all societies where it cometh. It maketh all men's goodness seem little, except our own; it causeth the people to undervalue their pastors, and turneth compassion of men's weakness into a sour contempt; it setteth a man, in his own conceit, so near to God, that he looketh down on other men as earthly animals in comparison of himself; it maketh new terms of church communion, and teacheth men to make narrower the door of the church, than God hath made it; it causeth men to deny and villify [*sic*] God's grace, in those that answer not their expectations, and to think that the church is not worthy of their communion; and to think that none are so fit as they to be the reformers of the church and of the world. I entreat those who are in danger of this pernicious sin, to think with themselves, 1. What a heinous crime and folly it is for one that but lately was a child of the devil, and a sink of sin, to be proud so quickly of his goodness; and for one that so lately was groaning and weeping with a broken heart, for a sinful life, to be already puffed up with the conceits of godliness; and for one who daily maketh confession to God of a sinful heart and a faulty life, and of great unworthiness, to contradict all this by an overvaluing of his own piety. And what an odious self-contradiction it is, to make yourself like the devil in pride, because you think you are like God in holiness!

2. Consider that the more you are proud of your goodness, the less you have to be proud of. If this sin be predominant, it is certain that you have no saving grace at all. And what an odious thing and miserable case is it, to be proud of holiness, when you are un-

holy; and to be damned both for the want of it, and for being proud of it: that a man should be proud of that, for want of which he must suffer the fire of hell! But if your pride be not predominant, yet it is certain that in what measure soever you have this pride, in that measure you are destitute of grace; for true grace and pride are as contrary as life and death.

3. And study well the meaning of all these scriptures, (for you shall not say that I misinterpret them to you:) Why was it that Christ mentioneth the parable of the Pharisee and the publican? one thanking God that he was not so bad as others, and the other thinking himself unworthy to look up to heaven. Luke xviii, 10, 11, &c. Why did he give us the parable of the prodigal, who confessed that he was unworthy to be called a son; and of his elder brother, who swelled with envy at his entertainment? Why was it that Christ seemed not strict enough to the Pharisees in keeping the sabbath, nor in his diet, nor in his company; but they called him a gluttonous person, and a wine-bibber, and a friend of publicans and sinners? Was it not because their pride and superstition made them think too highly of their own religiousness; and to make sins and duties which God never made, and then to condemn the innocent for want of this human religiousness? What was the sin condemned in Isaiah lxv, 5, which says, "Stand by thyself, come not near to me; for I am holier than thou?" What meaneth that command in Phil. ii, 3, "Let nothing be done through strife, or vain-glory; but in lowliness of mind let each esteem other better than themselves?" Read this verse over upon your knees, and beg of God to write it on your hearts; and join with it Rom. xii, 10: "Be kindly affectioned one to another with brotherly love, in honour preferring one another;" that is, before yourselves. But especially read and study James iii. In a word, if God would cure the church of religious pride— the pride of wisdom, and the pride of piety and

goodness— the church would have fewer heresies and contentions, and have much more peace, and much more true wisdom and goodness in itself.

Direction III.

Overvalue not the common gift of utterance, nor a high profession, as if the presence or absence of either of them did prove the presence or absence of grace.

Yet neither of these must be undervalued, nor accounted needless, useless things. But the overvaluing them hath caused great distempers in the minds and affections, and communion and practice, of many very well-meaning Christians. When God had first brought me from among the more ignorant sort of people, and when I first heard religious persons pray without forms, and speak affectionately and seriously of spiritual and heavenly things, I thought verily that they were all undoubted saints; and the sudden apprehension of the difference of their gifts and speech from others, made me think confidently that the one sort had the mark of God upon them, and the other had nothing almost of God at all: till, ere long, many of those whom I so much honoured, began to discover an unscriptural disposition. But the experience of this kingdom these twenty-six years, hath done so much to convince the world what crimes may stand with high professions, that I know not that I ever met with the man that would deny it: seeing every sect casteth it upon all the rest, however some of them would justify themselves. But I greatly fear, lest the generation which is now springing up, and knew not those men, nor their miscarriages, will lose the benefit of these dreadful warnings, and scarce believe what high professors did prove the proudest overturners of all government; and resisters and despisers of ministry and holy order in the churches, and the most railing Quakers, and the most filthy and blaspheming ranters; to warn all the world to take heed of being proud of superficial gifts and high professions; and that he that standeth in his own conceit, should take heed lest he fall.

When gifts of utterance in prayer or talking are thus overvalued, and high professions are taken to have more in them than they have, men presently model their affections, and then the church, according to their misconceivings; and a talkative person, who by company and use hath got more of these gifts than better Christians, shall be extolled and admired, when many an humble, upright soul, that wanteth such utterance, shall be said to be no professor, and so to be unworthy of the communion of saints. Mistake me not; I know that though profession may be without sincerity, yet sincerity cannot be without some profession, when there is opportunity to make it: and I know that grace is a vital principle, and like fire which will work, and seek a vent if you would restrain it; and that gifts of utterance are great mercies of God, for the edification of the church. But here lieth your unhappy error in this case; you take a moderate profession of Christianity to be no profession at all, because there is wanting a profession of greater zeal and forwardness: whereas you should make proper allowance for constitutions and circumstances.

In the place where I exercised my ministry, I found some gave me a satisfying evidence in their last sickness that they had long lived a truly godly life, who were never noted by their neighbours for any extraordinary zeal at all. If you ask me, How can it stand with grace to be so much hid? I answer, they made a profession of Christianity; they usually attended the public worship; they lived blamelessly in their places: but they were of silent, retired dispositions, and were inferiors, who by their superiors were restrained from private meetings, and some converse with more zealous persons, which they desired. And for aught you know, there may be very many such, who must not be rejected as no professors, without a particular accusation and proof, unless you would be used in the like kind yourselves.

Direction IV.

Affect not to be made eminent and conspicuous in holiness, by standing at a further distance from these lower professors than God would have you. It is the loathsome scab of the Romish Church, that they who will be taken for religious must go into a monastery of friars and nuns, and separate themselves from the rest of Christians as worldly, secular people, that so their religion may be a noted thing, and they may be set up in their singularity as public spectacles for the world to admire; though, perhaps, they come thither but under the gripes of conscience, to expiate the guilt of whoredom, murder, or some notorious sins, which the contemned seculars never committed.

Many a one who perceiveth how childish a thing it is to set out one's self to be observed for fine clothes, or for bodily comeliness, or for high entertainments, curiosities, houses, lands, or such vanities, doth yet think that it is an excellent thing to be honoured by men, especially by the wisest and the best, as a person of wisdom, and piety, and goodness. And, indeed, it is the truest and highest honour to be wise and good; and it is exceeding natural to man to desire honour, and it is lawful to have a religious regard to our honour. And this being so, how easy it is for pride to take this advantage, and to go a little farther, while we think we go but thus far and keep within our bounds.

Direction V.

Search the Scriptures with diligence and prayer. Many are very sensible of the need of spirituality and seriousness in religion, and of the evil of hypocritical formality and imagery, and of usurpation of the prerogatives of Christ, and of the plague of persecuting pride and cruelty, who yet have little sense at all of the good of unity, and of the mischiefs of divisions in the church. Yea, many are so careful to be found exact in their obedience to God, that they build very much, for duties and against sins, upon dark and very far-fetched consequences, and upon a few obscure and doubtful passages in Scripture, when there is no express words, or clear text at all, to bear them out: and, doubtless, the darkest intimations of the will of God must not be disregarded. But, on the other side, we cannot bring them to lay to heart some duties and sins, which are over and over a hundred times, and that with vehemency, expressed and argued in the plainest words.

And because all Christians pretend to submit to the word of God, I will try whether it be not thus with you in the present case, and will cite many plain expressions of Scripture, for Christian unity and concord, that, you may either better perceive your duty, or plainly show your great partiality.

Zechariah iv, 9; Ezekiel xxxiv, 23; xxxvii, 22, 24; Jeremiah xxxii, 39; Ezekiel xi, 19; John xi, 52; xxi, 22; Acts i, 14; ii, 1; iv 24, 32; v, 12; xv, 25; 2 Corinthians xi, 2; Ephesians iv, 1, 12, 13; 1 Corinthians xii, 3, 12, 13, 15, 22, 23; xiii, 4, 5, 13; i, 10, 12, 13; iii, 3, 4, 15; Romans xiv, 1, 3, 10, 13, 14, 17; xv, 1, 2, 5, 6; xvi, 17, 18; Acts xx, 30; John xiii, 35; 1 Corinthians xi, 17, 18; Matthew xiii, 29, 30, 41, 47; xxii, 9, 10; Luke xiv; Galatians vi, 1; Philippians i, 15, 16; ii, 1, 2, 3, 14; iii, 15, 16; 1 Thessalonians v. 12, 13; Titus iii, 10; James iii, 1, 2, 13, &c; Matt. xii, 25.

I have cited so many texts against division, and for the unity of the church and concord of Christians, as one would think the very hearing of them, without exposition or argumentation, should utterly mortify all inclinations to divisions and hard censures, in all true believers: yea, so many texts as I am persuaded many that most need them, will think it tedious to look for and to read them over. And yet I have cause to fear, lest many such will feel as little of the sense and authority of them, as if there were no such words in the Scripture, and none of this had been set before them.

Out of all these you may gather these reasons of the necessity of unity, and of the evil of schism or division. It is one end and happiness which we all expect; and one heaven that we must meet and live in for ever, (so many as are sincere in the faith which we profess:) and in heaven we shall have one mind and heart, and one employment in the love and praise of our Creator and Redeemer, and one felicitating fruition of his glory for evermore. Therefore he that seeth not the necessity of unity, knoweth not the nature of the church, or faith, or true religion.

An army is stronger than a man; and a kingdom than a single person. A flame will burn more strongly than a spark; and the waves of the ocean are more forcible than a single drop. A threefold cord is not easily broken. Therefore it is that commonwealths do seek to strengthen themselves by confederacies with other states. The church is like to an army with banners; both for their numbers, their concord, and their order. And therefore Christ saith that a kingdom divided cannot stand. Union is the church's strength. And what good soever they may pretend, dividers are certainly the weakeners and destroyers of the church. And as those means which best corroborate the body, and fortify the spirits, do best cure many particular diseases which no means would cure while nature is debilitated; so are the church's diseases best cured by uniting, fortifying remedies, which will be increased by a dividing way of reformation. Dividing is wounding; and uniting is the closing of the wound. There is no good work but Satan is a pretender to it, when he purposeth to destroy it. He resisteth light as an angel of light; and his ministers hinder righteousness, as pretended ministers of righteousness. And he will be a zealous reformer, when he would hinder reformation. And this is the mark of Satan's way of reformation: he doth it by dividing the church of Christ, and teaching Christians to avoid each other. And to that end he zealously aggravateth the faults of every party to the rest, that they may have odious thoughts of one another; and Christian love may be turned into aversion. As in the plague time every one is afraid of the breath and company of his neighbour; and they that were wont to assemble, and converse with peace and pleasure, do timorously shun the presence of each other, because they know that it is an infectious time, and they are uncertain who is free; even so doth Satan break the societies and converse of Christians, by making them believe that there is some dangerous infection, which, as they love their souls, they must avoid. And he destroyeth your love to one another, by pretending love for yourselves. O how careful will he be for your souls! When the Devil would undo you, he will do it as your saviour: and when his meaning is to save you from heaven, and from Christ, and from his saving grace, and from union and communion with his church, and from the impartial love of one another, he takes on him that he is saving you only from sin, and from church corruptions; or rather that it is Christ, and not he, that giveth you counsel: and he can do much in imitating Christ, in the manner of his suggestions, to make you believe that it is Christ indeed. Perhaps his counsel shall come in the midst of a *fervent prayer*, or presently after it, to make you believe that it is an undoubted answer of your prayers. And oftentimes his impulses are vehement, and much affecting, to make you think that it is something above nature: and the pious pretence will much persuade you to think that sure this can never come from an evil spirit. But if you had well studied 2 Cor. xi, 13-15; Gal. i, 8; Luke ix, 55; 1 John iv, 1, 2; 2 Thess. ii, 2;

you might be wiser, and be saved from this deceit. I will not recite the words; because I would have you turn to them, and seriously study them.

Remember also, that the unity of Christians is their peace and ease, as well as their strength and safety. Psalm cxxxiii, 1: "Behold, how good and pleasant it is for brethren to dwell together in unity!"

As the amity and converse with friends is pleasant, and the concord of families is their quietness and ease; so it is as to that amity and concord which is the bond of church society: and the divisions and discord of Christians is their mutual pain and trouble. Do you not feel your minds disturbed by it? Do you not see the church discomposed by it? The itch of contention doth ordinarily make it pleasant for the time, to scratch by zealous wranglings and disputes for their several opinions, till the blood be ready to follow: but the smart and scab doth use to convince them of their folly. But if they will go more than skin deep, they may need a surgeon. Children will claw themselves; but it is madmen that will wound themselves. The hurt which we get in the Christian warfare, by mortifying the flesh, or by the persecution of the malignant enemy, is tenderly healed by the hand of Christ, and usually furthereth our inward peace. But if we will hurt and wound ourselves, what pity or comfort can we expect?

Consider also that the unity and concord of believers is their honour, and their divisions and discord are their shame: and consequently the honour or dishonour of Christ, and the gospel, and religion, is much concerned in it. Agreement among Christians telleth the world that they have a certainty of the faith which they profess, and that it is powerful, and not ineffectual; and that it is of a healing nature, and tendeth to the felicity of the world. But divisions and discords among Christians persuade unbelievers that there is no certainty in their belief; or that it is of a vexatious and destructive tendency; or at best that all its power is too weak to overcome the malignity which it pretendeth to resist. Where did you ever see Christians live in undivided unity, undisturbed peace, and unfeigned love, but the very infidels and ungodly round about them, did reverence them and their religion for it? And where did you ever see Christians divided, unpeaceable, and bitter against each other, but it made them and their profession a scorn to the unbelieving and ungodly world? And while they despise and villify [sic] one another, they teach the wicked to despise and villify them all.

Peace and concord are amiable even to nature. And you can scarce take a more effectual means to win the world to the love of holiness, than by showing them that holiness doth make you unfeigned and fervent in the love of one another. 1 Pet. i, 22. Nor can you devise how to drive men more effectually from Christ, and to damn their souls, than to represent Christians to them like a company of madmen, that are tearing out the throats of one another. How can you think that the unbelievers and ungodly should think well of them that all speak so ill of one another?

External unity and peaceable church communion doth greatly cherish our internal unity of love: and church divisions do cherish wrath and malice, and all the works of the flesh described by Paul, Gal. v, 21-23. I pray you consider how he describeth the fleshly and spiritual man, ver. 14, 15: "For all the law is fulfilled in one word, even in this, Thou shalt love thy neighbour as thyself. But if ye bite and devour one another, take heed that ye be not consumed one of another. I say then, Walk in the Spirit, and ye shall not fulfil the lusts of the flesh: for the flesh lusteth against the Spirit," &c. "Now the works of the flesh are manifest: — adultery, enmities or hatred, variance, emulations, wrath, strife, seditions, (or, as it may be read, divisions or factions,) heresies, envyings, murders, &c. But the fruit of the Spirit is love, joy, peace, long-suffering, gentleness, goodness, faith, meekness, temperance: against such there is no law. And they that are Christ's have crucified the flesh, with the affections and lusts. If we live in the Spirit, let us also walk in the Spirit; let us not be desirous of vain- glory, provoking one another, envying one another."

Objection. O, but those I complain of are guilty of this, that, and the other fault.

Answ. Chap. vi, 1: "Brethren, if a man be overtaken in a fault, ye which are spiritual restore such a one in the spirit of meekness; considering thyself lest thou also be tempted." Instead of censorious disdain and separation, "bear ye one another's burden, and so fulfil the law of Christ:" which you think you fulfil by your unwarrantable conduct, while you are but fulfilling your fleshly passions. When once parties are engaged by their opinions in fierce disputings, the flesh and Satan will be working in them against all that is holy, sweet, and safe. When uniting Christians are provoking one another to love and to good works, and minding each other of their heavenly cohabitation and harmonious praise; and are delighting God and man by the melody of their concord; the contentious zealots are preaching down love, and preaching up hatred, and making those that differ from them seem an odious people not to be borne with. James iii, 1, &c.: "My brethren, be not many teaching masters, (for this is the word,) knowing that we shall receive the greater condemnation: for in many things we offend all. If any man offend not in word, the same is a perfect man;" that is, if you will show that you are perfect, and better yourselves than those whom you account so bad, see that your foul, backbiting, reviling, censorious, contentious tongues, do not prove the contrary. Ver. 13: "Who is a wise man and endued with knowledge among you? let him show out of a good conversation his works with meekness of wisdom;"

that is, let him that will be thought more knowing and religious than his neighbours, be so much more blameless and meek to all men, and excel in good works. Verse 14: "But if you have a bitter zeal (for so is the Greek word) and strife in jour hearts, glory not," — in such a zeal, or in your greater knowledge, — "and lie not against the truth." Verse 15: "This wisdom descendeth not from above," (as you imagine who father it on God's word and Spirit,) "but is earthly, sensual, or natural and devilish." O doleful mistake, that the world, the flesh, and the devil, should prove the cause of that conceited spiritual knowledge and excellency, which they thought had been the inspiration of the Spirit! Verse 16: "For where zeal and strife is," (that is, a striving, contentious zeal against brethren,) "there is confusion," (or tumult and unquietness,) "and every evil work." O lamentable reformers, that set up every evil work, while they seem zealous against evil! Verse 17: "But the wisdom that is from above is first pure, then peaceable, gentle, and easy to be entreated; full of mercy and good fruits; without partiality," (or wrangling,) "and without hypocrisy. And the fruit of righteousness is sown in peace, of them that make peace;" when peace-breakers that sow contention shall reap the fruit of unrighteousness, though they call their way by the most religious names.

Resolve with Austin, I will not be the chaff; and yet I will not go out of the floor, though the chaff be there. Never give over your just desire and endeavour of reformation; and yet, as long as possibly you can avoid it, forsake not those who, as you suppose, are in some things wrong. As Paul said to them that were ready to forsake a sea-wrecked vessel, "If they abide not in the ship, ye cannot be saved." Many a one by unlawful flying, and shifting for his own greater peace and safety, doth much more hazard his own and others. Many weak Christians, marking those texts which bid us avoid a man that is a heretic, and have no company with disorderly walkers, and not to eat with flagitious persons, do not sufficiently mark their sense; but take them as if they called us to separate from the church with which these persons do communicate. Whereas, if you mark all the texts in the gospel, you shall find that all the separation which is commanded in such cases, (besides our separation from the infidels, or idolatrous world, or antichristian and heretical confederacies,) is but one of these two sorts: first, either that the church cast out the impenitent sinner by the power of the keys; or, secondly, that private men avoid all private familiarity with them. And both these we would promote, and no way hinder.

But that the private members should separate from the church, because such persons are not cast out of it, show me one text to prove it, if you can.

Let us here peruse the texts that speak of our withdrawing from the wicked. 1 Cor. v, is expressly written to the whole church, as obliged "to put away the incestuous person from among them, and so not to eat with such offenders." So is that in 2 Thess. iii, and that in Tit. iii, 10: "A man that is an heretic, after the first and second admonition avoid." Unless it be an heretic that hath already separated himself from our communion; and then it can be but private familiarity which we are farther to avoid. In brief, there is no other place of Scripture, that I know of, which commandeth any more. The apostle never spake a syllable to any one Christian, to separate from any one of all those churches; which we cannot imagine the Holy Ghost would have wholly omitted, if it had been the will of God. Here are two things which I desire you to observe: First, what is Christ's appointed way for removing members from the communion of the church. Secondly, how great a sin it is to remove them by a contrary and arbitrary way of our own presumptuous invention.

First. It is supposed that the person is not a professed

apostate: for there needeth no *casting out* of such. He that turneth *Turk* or *heathen*, or openly renounceth Christianity, or ceaseth the profession of it, doth go out of the church himself, and needeth not be *cast* out. Unless it be a tyrant who will come to the communion in scorn, while he professeth but to show his lawless will. He that seeketh the communion of the church in sobriety, thereby professeth himself a Christian: and Christ's way of rejecting such is plainly described in the gospel. Matt. xviii, 15, 16; Titus iii, 10; 1 Cor. v, 7, 11-13.

By all this it is plain that the church must exercise a regular course of justice, with every person that it shall reject. He must first be told *privately* of his fault, and then before two or three; (unless, at least, the open notoriety make the private admonition needless.) And then it must be told the church: and the church must with compassion, tenderness, and patience, and yet with the authority of the Lord Jesus, and the powerful evidence of truth, convince him and persuade him to repent; and he must not be rejected, till, after all this, he obstinately refuse to hear the church; that is, to repent, as they exhort him.

Note also, that no private person may expect that any offender be cast out, either because his sin is known to him, or because he is commonly famed to be guilty, till the thing be proved by sufficient witness. Yea, the admonition given him must be proved, as well as the fault which he committed. Yea, if all the town do know him to be guilty, and witness prove that he hath been privately admonished, he may not be rejected, till he be heard to *speak for himself,* and till he refuse also the regular admonition.

This is Christ's order, whose *wisdom*, and *mercy*, and *authority*, are such, as may well cause us to take his way as best. And yet the ignorance or rashness of many professors is such, that they would have all this order of Christ overturned: and some of them must have such persons kept away and rejected, before ever they have admonished them, or exhorted them to repentance, or proved that any one else hath done it; much more before they have told the minister, or proved that he hath neglected the minister's admonition.

The sinfulness of unchurching persons, without Christ's way of regular process, consisteth in all these following parts: —

1. It is a casting off the laws of the great Lawgiver of the church, and so a contempt of his authority, wisdom, and goodness; and a making of ourselves *greater*, or *wiser*, or *holier*, than he.

2. It is gross injustice to deprive men of so great privileges without any sufficient proof of their forfeiture.

3. And it is an aggravated crime in them, that so much cry down *church tyranny* in others, to be thus notoriously guilty of it themselves. What greater injustice and tyranny can there be, than that men's Christianity and church rights shall be judged null, upon the censures and rumours of suspicious men, without any just proof or lawful trial? That it shall be in the power of every one who hath uncharitableness enough to think evil of his neighbours, or to believe reports against their innocency, to cast them out of the family of God, and to unchristian and unchurch men arbitrarily at their pleasure? That any man, who in the heat of his spirit is but unreasonable enough to say, "They are *ignorant* or *profane*," shall expect to have his neighbours excommunicated?

4. It maketh all churches to be lubricous and uncertain shadows, when a censorious person may unchurch them at his pleasure. What you say of others, another may say of you, and as justly expect to be believed.

5. It unavoidably bringeth in incurable *divisions*; for there is no certain rule of justice with such persons; and, therefore, they know not who are to be received to their

communion, and who not. And the same man that one will think ought to be rejected and kept out, another will think is to be received.

And let it be well observed, the power of baptizing is the power *of the keys* for *reception into* the church. The private members have not the power of *baptizing*, nor were the pastors ever appointed to do it by their advice, consent, or vote. Therefore, the private members have not the power of the keys for admission; and it is most apparent in the gospel that the keys for *admission* and for *exclusion* are given into the same hands, and not one to the ministers and another to the flock: therefore, the people that have not the first, have not the latter. For full proof of this, observe the meaning of these texts:— Isa. xxii, 22; ix, 6; Matt. xvi, 19; xviii, 18; John xx, 23. Matt. xxviii, 19; John xx, 21; Acts i, 16, 17; xx, 28; Rom. i, 1; 1 Cor. iv, 1; Acts xiv, 23; Titus i, 3, 7. 1 Tim. iii, 5; v, 17; 1 Pet. v, 2; Heb, xiii, 7, 17, 24; 1 Thess. v, 12, 13. Read these with judgment, and then believe, if you can, that the power of the keys or government is in the people. Show us what text doth give them that power. And where the Scripture calleth them to exercise it by votes. Or where he calleth them to leave their callings, and attend this work. When those that must perform it, he separateth to it as by office, and calleth to *give themselves wholly* thereto. 1 Tim. iv, 15, 16. Tell us when the people were authorized to baptize, or to rule the church; that is, themselves.

Objection. In Matt. xviii, 15: "Tell the church; if he hear not the church," &c. Answ. Many expositors think that by the *church there* is meant the ministers only; by this reason,— The church that must *teach* must be *heard*; the church that must be *heard* must be *told*: but that is only the pastors and not the people. *Ergo*— But suppose I grant you, that the word [*church*] there signifieth the whole congregation, (as Dr. Taylor sayeth in his second dissuasive,) yet it is an organized body only; and so the office is to be performed only by the organical part, and not by any of the rest. When I say to a man, "Hear me;" I do not mean that he should hear me with his eyes, but only with his ears. And when I bid him *see* or *read*, I bid him not to do it with his *ears*, but with his *eyes*. Nor do the eyes receive this power from the feet or hands, but immediately from the head: though if they were separated from the body, they could not retain it. Objection. 1 Cor. v: Paul biddeth all the church *to put from among them that wicked person*. Answ. Note that Paul passed the sentence first himself, [*I have judged as if I were present* (not that *you deliver*, but) to deliver such a one to Satan,] and, therefore, doth this himself *in the name of the Lord Jesus*, and supposeth himself *among them in spirit and power*, when they do it [*and my spirit with the power of our Lord Jesus Christ.*]

2. And I have said, he speaketh to an organized church, which had two parts, and accordingly two works to do. The *ruling* part was to *put away the offender* by *judgment*, or *sentence*; and the people were all to *put him away*, by actual *shunning* his communion; which is but the obeying that sentence. If the king send to a corporation to execute any law, he meaneth not that *all persons* must do it in the like manner; but the magistrates by command, and the people by obeying them, and executing their commands. If I desire a man to transcribe me a book, and bring it me; I mean not that every part of him shall herein have the same office: but that he *read* it only with his *eyes*, and understand it with his *reason*, and transcribe it with his *hand*, and travel with his *feet*. The pastors only excommunicate by judgment or sentence, and the people by obedient execution.

Farther you are not at all bound *to know* what the spiritual state of any man is, as he is to join in church communion with you, but upon your *pastor's trust* and *word*.

Whether their understanding be sufficient at their admittance, you are not anywhere called to try: but the pastor is: and if he have admitted them, you are to rest in his judgment, unless you would undertake the office yourself. Whether their profession of faith and repentance be serious and credible, you are not called to try and judge; but if your pastor have admitted them, he hath numbered them with the visible church; and it is the *credibility* of the *pastor* that you have to consider; and by him you must judge of the credibility of the professor, and not immediately by your own trial. Who are the persons that you shall meet at a sacrament or in public communion you are not at all required to try; and if you never saw them before, or heard them speak, you may perform your duty nevertheless; indeed, if as a *neighbour* you are called to instruct, or counsel, or comfort them, you must do it: but there may be five thousand in one church with you, whose names or faces you are not bound to know; but to rest in the knowledge of them to whom the keys are committed, who according to their office take them in.

Objection. *But what if they are notoriously wicked? must I be blind?*

Answ. No. You must do your best, by neighbourly watchfulness and help, (though not by pastoral government,) to reform all about you to whom you are able to do good. And if you know them to be so bad, you must privately admonish them, as is proved: and then if they hear not, tell the minister. But if you see a man in the church at the sacrament, or a thousand men, who are unreformed, and you know it not, you have no reason to avoid the communion of such. And if there be a thousand in the church whose case you are strangers to, this may be no sin of yours; and should be no impediment of your communion.

Objection. *But will it not be my sin, if I communicate*

*with such as I know to be wicked; when a little leaven
leaveneth the lump?*

Answ. It will be your sin, if you obey not Christ (Matt.
xviii, 15) in admonishing them; and so if it be through
you that they are not removed. But otherwise, if they be
there without your fault, it is no more your sin to communicate with such men, than it is to live and converse
with fellow-servants that are wicked; when it is not *you*,
but your *master*, that hath the choice of them. And the
leavening of the *lump*, of which the text speaketh, is the
tempting of others to the like sin; and not that the innocent shall be held guilty. Christ's outward discipline is
agreeable to his inward. As those that *come to him by faith*,
he will in no wise cast out or reject; so those that come to
him by *profession* of faith, he will not have his ministers
in any wise reject. And *coming to Christ* when he was
personally on earth, did signify the following of him, as
well as believing in him; just so far as men will come, so
far they shall be received by Christ: if they will come but
toward him, he will not put them back. If they will come
but to his *visible church* by a dead profession, he would
not have his ministers repulse them as long as their lives
are moral. The outward privileges of the visible church
which they come to, they shall possess. If they will come
over to the church of the regenerate, they shall be saved.
But wherever they stop, it shall be their own doing. Many
came to Christ when he was on earth, whom he never
repulsed, though he was marvelled at and grudged at for
entertaining them. Some came so far as to own his name,
and did miracles by it, that yet did not follow him: whom
the apostles would have hindered, but Christ reproved
them. Mark ix, 38; Luke ix, 49. Some came only to receive a cure of their diseases from him, whom his disciples sometimes repulsed, but so did not he. When little
children were brought to him, his disciples rebuked them
that brought them, as thinking them unfit for his recep-

tion; but Christ rebuked them for their forbidding of such guests. When he eat and drank with publicans and sinners, and when he received a kindness from a woman that had been a great sinner, the Pharisees censured him therefore, as ungodly; but yet he would not abate his clemency. And though Simon Magus would not come out of the gall of bitterness and bond of iniquity, yet was he not kept out of the visible church, when he professed to believe, and desired baptism.

Indeed, if men will not come so far as to the *profession of true faith or repentance*, they are not to be received into the church, because the church is a society of *such professors*; and if they will not come, they cannot be received. But if Christians had well studied the compassions of a Saviour, and the tenor of his gospel, and his practice upon earth; and instead of a surly flying from their neighbours, and groundless censuring them, were possessed, themselves with that love and tenderness, which is the evangelical temper and the image of their Lord; it would put an end to many divisions, and bring us nearer the truth and one another.

It is far from the mind of Christ that no difference should be made between the *holy* and *profane*, the precious and the vile; or that serious piety should be suppressed or discouraged; or faithful preachers hindered from promoting it; or ignorant, graceless ministers, countenanced—under pretence of *peace* or *order*. The design of Christ was not like Mohammed's, to get himself an earthly kingdom and numerous followers, merely to cry up his name; and therefore he will not indulge men in their sins, nor abate or alter the conditions of the covenant to win disciples. He will have his ministers deal plainly with all to whom they preach, and let them know, that without *self-denial* and *forsaking all*, (in estimation and resolution,) and a willing exchange of earth for heaven, they cannot be his true disciples; nor without a *professed consent* to thus much, they cannot be his *visible professed* disciples: but all that will not repent must perish. His ministers also must impartially exercise the keys which he hath committed to their trust, and must not fear the faces of men, who at most are able but to kill the body. Luke xii, 4. They must discern between the righteous and the wicked; and draw all scandalous sinners to repentance, or else exclude them from the communion of the saints, that the world may see that Christ is no friend to profane persons, or sensual fleshly brutes. If you meet a profane person at the Lord's table, it is your own fault or the pastor's: but if you keep company needlessly with such, or marry such, it is your own fault altogether. If the pastor do not excommunicate them, you may choose not to be familiar with them. Though you meet them at the church, and pray with them; you need not meet them at other places, and drink with them. Though you may not with a few of the most godly separate from the public communion of all the rest; yet you may keep a more intimate familiarity with those few than with all the rest. And if you will consider, this is all that is necessary to your own duty, and that which is best for your own edification. Keep thus to a strictness within the bounds of your own place and calling, and God will bless you in such a strictness.

The teachings, commands, exhortations, and reproofs of God, are directed to the *will* of man; and the promises and threatenings, mercies and judgments, are used to move and change the will: and in the tenor of his laws and covenants, Christ hath set life and death before men, and put their *happiness* in their own choice; and no man shall have better or worse than he made choice of— that is, none shall be either happy or miserable, but as they did *choose* or *refuse* the causes of happiness or misery. And the reason of this is, because natural free will was a part of the *natural image* of God on Adam; and it is as natural to a man to be a *free agent,* as to be reasonable. And God

will govern *man* as *man*, agreeably to his nature. Therefore do not wonder if church privileges are principally
left to men's own wills or choice, when their salvation is
left to it. And for us to grudge at this order of God, is but
to quarrel at wisdom and goodness, and to correct God's
order by our disorder. The man that came in without a
wedding-garment, is blamed, and bound hand and foot,
and punished: but the minister that called him in, and
admitted him, is not blamed; because he knew not his
hypocrisy, but did as he was bidden: he went to the high-
ways and hedges, and compelled them by importunity
to come in, that the house might be filled. Nor were any
that came in with him blamed, for having communion
with such. For they were in their places, and did as they
were exhorted to do. And so will it be in the case that is
before us.

Direction VI.

Beware of being governed by YOUR PASSIONS. We are seldom more mistaken in justifying ourselves than in our
passions; and when our *passions* are *religious*, the mistake is both most easy and most perilous. Easy, because
we are apt to be most confident, and not suspect them,
the matter seeming so great and good about which they
are exercised; and perilous, because the greatness and
goodness of the matter doth make the error the greater
and the worse. I have showed before how easy it is to
think that our religious passions are all the works of the
Spirit of God; for we are apt to estimate them by the depth
and earnestness which we feel. But excellent persons have
been here mistaken, as James and John were. And not
only so, but when the passion is up, the judgment itself is
seldom to be trusted; for it inclineth us to err in all things
that concern the present business. Therefore, still remember the difference between true zeal and false; and know
that he that is upright in the main, and whose zeal for

Christianity is sound, may yet have much zeal that is unsound with it.

First. It is an ill sign when your zeal is raised about some singular opinion which you have owned, and not for the common salvation and substance of the Christian faith or practice; or at least when your odd opinion hath a greater proportion of your zeal than many more plain and necessary truths.

Secondly. When your zeal is moved by any *personal interest* of your own: by honour or dishonour; by any wrong that is done you; or any reputation of wisdom or goodness which lieth on the cause; or at least when your *own interest* hath too large a proportion in your zeal.

Thirdly. When your zeal is more for the interest of your adherents than for the church, and the common cause of godliness and Christianity, and can be content that some detriment to the whole may further the interest of you and your adherents.

Fourthly. When your zeal tendeth to hurt and cruelty, and would have God rather to glorify his *justice* by some present notable judgment, than his mercy by patience and forgiving: and when your secret desire of *fire from heaven*, or some destruction of the adversaries, is greater than your desire and prayer for their conversion. The sure mark of true zeal is, that it is zealous love: it maketh you love your neighbours and enemies more fervently than others do; but false zeal maketh you more inclined to their suffering, and to reproach them.

Fifthly. It is an ill sign when your zeal is beyond the proportion of your understanding; and your *prudence* and *experience* are as much less than other men's, as your *zeal is greater*. True zeal hath some equality of *light* and *heat*.

Sixthly. It is an ill sign when it is a zeal which is easily kept alive, and hardly restrained: for that showeth the flesh and the devil are too much its friends. True zeal of the spirit doth need the fuel of all holy means, and the bellows of meditation and prayer to kindle it: and all is too little to keep it up in the constancy that we desire. But carnal zeal will burn of itself without such endeavours.

Seventhly. It is an ill sign when some *forward teacher* was the kindler of it; and not the sober preaching of the truth.

Eighthly. And it is an ill sign when it burneth in the same soul where *lust*, or *wrath*, or *pride*, or *malice*, burns; and when it prospereth at the same time when the love of God, and a heavenly mind and life, decay. The zeal of a sensualist, of a proud man, of a covetous man, of a self-conceited, empty person, can hardly be thought a spiritual zeal.

Ninthly. And it is an ill sign when it carrieth you from the holy rule; and pretendeth to come from a spirit which will not be tried by the Scripture: or when it driveth you to use means which God forbiddeth in his word; and putteth you upon ways which the sealed law and testimony condemn. It cannot be of God, if it is against God's word.

By all these signs you may easily perceive how dividing zeal doth differ from the genuine Christian zeal. The one is a zeal for some *singular opinion*: the other is a zeal for *godliness* and *Christianity*. The one is kindled by some interest of our own religious reputation: the other is kindled by the interest of the *will* and *glory of God*. The one is a burning, hurting zeal, even the same which hath made matter for so many martyrologies and frightful histories, by inquisitions, torments, prisons, flames, massacres, and bloody wars, and the same which has silenced so many faithful ministers, and disturbed so many states and churches: the other is a zeal of love, which maketh men fervent in doing good to others. The one causeth men to revile, and despise, and censure, and backbite, and zealously to make others seem odious, that the hearers may abate their love to them: the other maketh us value all that is good in others, and to hide their nakedness, and to make them better, and to provoke the hearers to love and to good works. The one tendeth to divisions, and sidings, and separations, and distances from our brethren; and to feed contentions: the other is a zeal for unity, amity, and peace. The one is the complexion of the weak and childish, the proud and self-conceited, the peevish and surly, sort of professors: the other is the zeal of solid knowledge, and of the prudent, humble, meek, and well-grounded sort of Christians. The one is a zeal which flieth most outward, against the sins of other men, and can live with pride, and covetousness, and selfishness, and sensuality, at home— such serve not the Lord Jesus, but their own bellies. Rom. xvi, 17, 18: the other beginneth at home, and consumeth all these vices in the heart; and as zeal increaseth, humility, meekness, love, self-denial, temperance, and heavenly-mindedness, increase. The one is easily got and easily kept, and hardly kept under! O how easy is it to get and keep a contemptuous, censorious, backbiting, dividing, or persecuting zeal! But the other is not so much befriended by Satan or the flesh, and, therefore, must be preserved by prayer and meditation, and very great diligence. How hard is it to keep up a zealous love of God and man, and a fervour in all our heavenly and spiritual desires! Abate but your diligence, and this will presently decay; when the fierce contending, hurting, separating, and persecuting zeal, doth need no such fuel or labour to maintain it. The one is kindled by the inflaming censures of some rash and passionate person, that knoweth better how to *kill love* than to *cause it*; or by the singular conceits of some divider; or by the backbitings of some *Doeg*, or malicious calumniator: the other is kindled by the humble and heavenly preaching of the gospel, and by meditations on Christ's example, and a study to imitate him and his saints in patience, forbearance, forgiving others, and doing good. The one is a zeal which carrieth men from the Scripture; to pretences of such revelations, inspirations, and impulses, as have no proof, but the feeling and fancy of the person; or, at least, to abuse the word of God, and plead it for that which is condemned — it provoketh men to some unlawful practice, under pretence of misinterpreted texts, and of good ends and meanings: the other still putteth you upon good, and striveth against evil, and goeth for trial of every cause to the law and to the testimony. And, lastly, the one is a zeal which pretendeth to have the Spirit, and yet goeth contrary to the common workings of the Spirit, in the most part of the best and wisest Christians: but the other is the common vital heat which animateth all the body of Christ, and actuateth all his living members; and keepeth up love and holiness in the church; and is the same in all humble, heavenly Christians, in the world. It will be of great use to you, in order to your own and the church's peace, to understand and observe the difference between these contrary sorts of religious zeal.

There are many women and passionate Christians who are earnest in prayer, but sometimes they run into this mistake, to judge ungroundedly of the answer of their prayers, by such conceits and strong apprehensions of their own, as never came from the Spirit of God at all. And it is a great wrong to God, to be made the author of man's infirmities and errors, and of that which is contrary to his word. And yet it is a very pitiful case as to the offenders; because it is usually the sin of persons that are very upright and honest in the main, and that are very serious in their prayers to God; and of such as have naturally such weakness of reason, and strength of affection, as that they are less *blameable*, though less curable, than others are.

There are very few that take their impulses and resolutions for the Spirit's answer of their prayers, but they had before an understanding most inclined to that opinion, or else a bias upon their affections, bending them that way; or something in themselves which occasioned the scales to turn that way.

Objection. "But I did bring my mind to a pure impartiality, and prayed to God that he would show me the truth, be it what it would: and that if this were not right, he would blast it, and never suffer it to go on; and the more I prayed, the more I was confirmed that this is the right."

Answ. All this may be, without any of God's approbation of the conclusion which you think is his answer to your prayers. For while you prayed that God would turn your mind from it, if it were not right; yet at that time your judgment was inclined to it, or your affections at least: and it is an easier thing to speak impartial words in prayer, than to get an impartial, unprejudiced mind. And when you think your mind is brought to an impartiality, alas! there may be many deep roots of prejudice which you observe not; and there is scarce one of a thousand, who thinketh that he prayeth with a pure impartiality, but his opinion, disposition, inclination, interest, or secret affection, doth bias and ponderate his mind more to one side than to the other. But if you were never so willing to know the truth, yet there are passions in you, and corruptions, and ignorance, and former errors, which may all do much to hinder you from knowing it; and may breed many false apprehensions in your mind; and yet you may cherish them with as dear an espousal and affection, as if they were certainly from God.

And moreover, you have been guilty of former sins; and whether God for any of them may leave you to run into mistakes, you know not; or whether any present self-conceitedness may occasion him to leave you to mistakes. But the principal part of my answer is this, God hath nowhere promised to reveal all his truth to you, because you desire him so to do. It is not every prayer of yours, which he hath promised to hear and grant; but only those which are agreeable to his will: his will is either his command or his promise.

You may not suppose that God will grant all the prayers which are put up in obedience to his commands: but only that you shall be no losers by such obedience; but he will give you that, or something which shall be as good for you. It may be God's command that godly children should pray for the lives of their sick parents; and that parents pray for the conversion of their ungodly children; and that we pray for all men: and yet it doth not follow that we shall have the very thing which we obediently pray for. But it is his *promising will* which is the measure of our *hope*, as his *commanding will* is the rule of our obedience. Whatever he hath promised he will certainly give us. Now God hath nowhere promised in his word that he will reveal the true meaning of every text of Scripture to every godly person that asketh it.

Praying is but one of the means which God hath appointed you to come to knowledge. Diligent reading, hearing, and meditation, and the counsel of the wisest, is another means; even to dig for it as for silver, and to search for it as for hidden treasure: and to continue so doing, and to wait at the posts of wisdom's doors, that knowledge may come into you by degrees and in time. God hath not promised you true understanding upon your prayers alone, without all the rest of his appointed means; nor that you shall attain it by those means, as soon as you desire and seek it: for then prayer would be a notable pretence for laziness, and they that would not be at the labour of study, meditation, or conference, might save all their pains, and go to God and ask wisdom of him, and he would give it them; even as idle beggars think without working to get an alms to maintain them in their slothfulness. If instead of all our reading, hearing, and meditation, we could but *pray*, and so get all the knowledge which other men study, labour, and wait for, it would be too cheap a way to wisdom. Solomon, that got it by prayer, commandeth us very great diligence to get it.

It is very considerable, not only that Christ increased in wisdom in his youth, but also that he would not enter upon his public ministry (as is aforesaid) till he was about thirty years of age. When it had been more easy for Christ to have got all knowledge by two or three earnest prayers, than for any of us.

Moreover you must pray according to God's *will of precept*, not only in the matter, but in the manner of your prayers. And there may be more selfishness, and many other corruptions in the manner of them, than you discern. And there are many things which with submission you may lawfully pray for, which God hath never promised you at all. You may pray for the life of the sick, and for the conversion and salvation of all your relations, and of thousands of others, which God will not give you. Otherwise all the relations of every true Christian should be saved, yea, and all his enemies, and all the world. To apply all this, It [*sic*] may be you are in doubt, whether this or the other be the meaning of such a text of Scripture. Or whether you should proceed in such a business, or should join in the use of such preaching and prayers, or not. And when you have prayed earnestly, you are confirmed *for* one way, and *against* the other. And perhaps all this is but to be confirmed in your error. For, first, you came with distempered affections; or with such a *fear* of going one way rather than the other, that the very *fear* doth much to cause your apprehensions. Or you came with the guilt of former sin. Or you have some partiality on your spirit, and a secret inclination to one side more than to the other; or some overvaluing of your own understanding, person, or prayers. Or you are lazy and presumptuous; and think God must teach you that in one hour, and at a wish or prayer, which others better than you must learn with prayer, and twenty years' study, diligence, and patience. Or you think God must needs resolve you in that which he never promised to resolve you in. Where hath he promised upon all your prayers that ever he will teach you in this life the sense of every text of Scripture? If ever he *promised* this, he will perform it. And is it to one Christian, or *to every praying Christian*, that he hath promised it? If to *every one*, why are we not *all of a mind*? Why be not all as wise as you? What need we commentaries then? Or what need have others of your revelations? If it be but to *some*, who be *those some*? And how shall we know them? And how know you that you are of them? And why do not those some condescend to write an infallible commentary upon all the Bible, when they themselves are taught it of God, that so we may doubt and differ no more.

But if you say that it is not the meaning of every text, that God hath promised to make known to you when you pray, but of some few, how will you know which those few be? And where is the promise which maketh this difference? Except only that to all Christians he hath promised to reveal so much as is necessary to their salvation. But if you will pray for more, your belief of your success must not go beyond the promise. If you will promise to yourselves, you must perform for yourselves.

Objection. "But hath not God bid us believe that we shall receive whatever we ask, and promised to believers that they shall receive it?"

Answ. He hath first made a law to command you to pray, and then made a promise to grant what you pray for according to his will, that is according to his command and promise; and hath made your believing of this promise one of the conditions of his fulfilling it to you. So that if you believe not his power and promise, you shall not have the thing promised. But if you pray and believe, and withal use those other means with diligence and patience, which God hath appointed, you shall know in that measure, as is suitable to your state, (for God hath not promised the same measure of knowledge to all true believers.) So that this is all that the promise giveth you, and not that you shall know all that you pray to know, and that immediately.

Objection. "But then you leave us at utter uncertainty whether we have the answer of our prayers or not."

Answ. Not so: but the answer of your prayers must not be tried by your conceits, but by God's rule. If you pray for that which you have neither a *command* nor *promise* for, your prayer is sin, and your answer can be nothing but God's rebuke, or your own delusion. But if you pray for that which you have a command for, but no particular promise, then you have only the general promise that your prayer shall not be lost, but shall bring down either the thing you pray for, or something else which the wisdom of God seeth to be best for you and others, and to his ends. And this is all that you can warrantably *believe*. But if you pray for that which hath both a command and a particular promise, (as the pardon of sin, and necessary grace and life eternal to a persevering believer) you may be sure that this prayer shall be granted in kind. So that you are not to judge of the answer of prayer by your conceit and passions, but by the promise of God, which you must believe will be fulfilled. Faith must tell you whether your prayers be accepted. Nay, if you should receive health, or wealth, or gifts, for yourselves or others, when you have prayed for them, you cannot tell whether it be a *merciful* answer to your prayer, or a *judgment*, unless you try it by faith according to the promise. I have nothing to say of the case of miracles, but this: If God promise a miracle, you may believe it because it is promised. If he perform it without a promise, then either you must not believe it till it is done, or else your faith must be a miracle also; and then the faith itself is its own justification. But miracles are now so rare, that all sober Christians will take heed how they expect them, or over hastily believe them; and especially how they take their own belief for a miracle. All the talk that some men make of a *particular faith* may be tried by what I have here said.

To conclude. The warning which I give you in this case is from long and sad experience. I have seen too many very honest-hearted Christians, especially *melancholy* persons, and *women*, who have been in great doubt about the opinions of the Millenaries, the Separatists, the Anabaptists, the Seekers, and such like: and, after earnest prayer to God, they have been strongly resolved for the way of error, and confident by the strong impression, that it was the Spirit's answer to their prayers; and thereupon they have set themselves into a course of sin. If you say, How know you that they were mistaken? I will tell you how. First. Because they have been resolved contrary to the word of God. And I know that God's Spirit did first make a standing rule to try all after-impulses by; and whatever impulse is contrary to that rule, is contrary to God's Spirit. The law and the testimony are now sealed, and all spirits to be tried by them. Isa. viii, 20. Secondly. Because I have found their impulses contrary to one another. One hath been resolved for infant baptism, and another against it. One hath had a revelation for prelacy, and another against all prelacy. One hath been confident of an answer of prayers for Antinomianism, and another for Arminianism. One for a public communion, and another to detest it: and both came in the same way. Thirdly. Because I have seen abundance of prophecies of things to come, (which people have this way received with the greatest confidence,) to prove all false. Fourthly. Because I have stayed till many of the persons have found by experience that they were deceived, and have confessed it with lamentation. And, fifthly, because, perhaps, I know more of the nature of prejudice, affection, melancholy, feminine weakness, and self-conceit, and of tempting God in the way of prayer, and of Satan's transforming himself into an angel of light, than every reader will know till they have paid for their learning, as I have done. Many that have no such impulses themselves, are yet so much taken with the reverence of others, that they are very apt to be seduced by their confidence. When so great a man as Tertullian was deceived by Montanus and his prophetess; when such a one as Hacket could deceive not only Coppinger and Arthington, but abundance more, some taking him for the Messiah, and some, by his breathing on them, thinking that they received the Holy Ghost; when David George, in Holland, and John of Leyden, in Munster, and Behmen Stiefelius, and so many more pretended prophets in Germany, could deceive so many persons as they did; when the pretended revelations of the Ranters first, and the Quakers after, could so marvellously transport many thousand professors of religion in this land: I think we have fair warning to take the counsel of St. John, "Believe not every spirit; but try the spirits, whether they be of God." It is a pitiful instance of the good, old, learned Commenius, who so easily believed the prophecies of Daubritius, and the rest which he hath published; yea, when he saw the prophecies fail, yet when he adjured the prophet to speak truth, and got him to swear as before the Lord that it was truth, this seemed enough to confirm his belief of him: whereas, if he had been as well acquainted with the nature of melancholy and hysterical passions as many others are, he would have known that as strange things as those he recorded of the man or woman, may be done without a divine inspiration. And that it is no wonder if that person swear that his words are true, who is first deceived himself before he deceive others. For a crack-brained person to believe his delusions to be real verities, is little wonder.

I have many a time myself conversed with persons of great honesty and piety, (though of no great judgment,) who have some of them affirmed that they had angelical revelations; and some of them thought that the Spirit of God did bring this scripture or that scripture to their mind in answer to their prayers, and to fix their religious opinions; and were so very confident that what they affirmed was the certain truth or voice of God, that I have been stricken with a reverence to their professions, and with a fear lest I should resist God in resisting them. But resolving to take none on earth for the master of my faith, but to try the spirits whether they be of God, by going to the law and testimony, I was constrained to turn my reverence into pity. For I found that their seeming revelations were some of them Scripture doctrine, and some of them contrary to the Scripture. As for that which is already in the Scripture, what need I further revelation for it? Is it not there sufficiently revealed? Can their words add any authority to the word of God? And have I not God's own ministers and means to help me to the knowledge of his word? And as for that which is *contrary* to Scripture, I am sure that it is contrary to the will of God; and if an angel from heaven should preach another gospel to me, I must hold him accursed. Gal. i, 7, 8. So that if these persons should have the appearance and voice of an angel speaking to them, I would despise it as well as the words of a mortal man, if they be against the recorded word of God.

But, by what I have seen and heard, I know that it is a great temptation to some weak Christians to hear one that is much in prayer say, Take heed what you do: have no communion in this or that way of worship; nor in this or that opinion; for I am sure it is against the mind of

God. I once thought as you do, but God hath better made known his mind unto me. But saving the due respect to the honesty of such persons, ask them, How shall I know that you are in the right? If they say, I will not reason the case with you, but I know it to be the mind of God; tell them that God hath made you reasonable creatures, and will accept no unreasonable service of you; and you have but one Master of your faith, even Christ: therefore, if they believe that themselves, which they can give you no reason to believe, they must be content to keep their belief to themselves, and not, for shame, persuade any other to it, without proof! If they say that God hath revealed it to them, tell them, that he hath not revealed it to you, till they prove their divine revelation. If God reveal it to them but for themselves, they must keep it to themselves. If he reveal it to them for others, he will enable them to make some proof of their revelations, that others may be sure that they sin not in believing them. If they say that the Scripture is their ground, tell them that the Scripture is already revealed to all; and if, indeed, what they speak be there, you are ready to believe it: but if they pervert the Scripture by false interpretation, or abuse of it, and misapply it, none of this is the work of the Spirit of God.

If they say that the Spirit hath told them the meaning of the Scripture, say as before, that is not told for you which is not proved to you. The Scripture is written in such words as men use, of purpose that they may understand it; and is to be sufficiently understood by all men that hear it, though they have no revelation. God hath also set pastors in his church to teach it; if, therefore, revelations be still necessary to the understanding of the Scripture revelations, then the Scriptures seem to be in vain; and these last revelations must again have new revelations to the right understanding of them also. The truth is, it is very ordinary with poor fanciful women, and melancholy persons, to take all their deep apprehensions for revelations. And if a text of Scripture come into their minds, they say, This text was brought to my mind, and that text was set upon my spirit: as if nothing could bring a text to their thoughts, but some extraordinary motion of God; and as if this bringing it to their mind would warrant their false exposition of it. To conclude. Decry not the necessity of the ordinary sanctifying work of the Spirit, to bless the Scripture to your true illumination and sanctification: but if they pretend to any other revelations or inspirations, or expositions of the Scriptures, which they cannot prove to you, despise them not, but modestly leave them to themselves; but take heed that the reverence of any one's holiness tempt you not to depart from the certain, sufficient word of God, and draw you not into any heresy, or separation, or opinion, contrary to God's standing law.

I have known some that have lived long in doubts and fears of damnation, who have turned Anabaptists, and suddenly had comfort: and yet in a short time they forsook that sect and turned to another. I have known those also that have lived many years in timorous complaints and fears of hell; and they have turned to the Antinomians, and suddenly been comforted. The reason of all this is plain to any judicious observer. 1. The persons are ignorant, and never had the right knowledge and skilful improvement of the sound doctrine, which at first they seemed to embrace; and, 2. The power of conceit and fancy brought them comfort or quietness in their change.

The novelty of the matter, and the greatness of the change, with the conceited excellency of the opinions and party, did make them think that they were now grown very acceptable to God. To this may be added, that as a life of holiness hath far more opposition from the devil, the world, and the flesh, than the changing of an opinion, or joining with a party hath; so it must be harder to get and keep that comfort which is got and kept by faith and holiness, than that which is got by such an easy change. We see among us what abundance of persons can live like beasts, in most odious whoredoms, drunkenness, and rage; or like devils, in bloody cruelty against the good; and yet be comforted because they are of the Church of Rome, which they think is the true church. As if God saved men for being of such a side or party! And why may not others easily take such kind of comfort? O, therefore, labour for well-grounded faith and solid knowledge, that you may attain the true evangelical comforts, and that your ignorance may not prepare you for deceit; and that you may not be like children tossed to and fro, and carried up and down with every wind of doctrine, by deceived and deceitful men: nor have need to go to the devil to be your comforter; nor to steal a little unlawful peace from parties and opinions, as if there were not enough to be had in Christ, and holiness, and eternal life.

Christ owneth no disciples which are not in one of these two ranks; either *teachers* by office upon a lawful call, or *learners* who submit to be taught by others. When his ministers have made men his disciples, they must afterward "teach them to observe all things whatsoever he hath commanded them." Matt. xxviii, 19, 20. And a learner must hear, and read, and discourse, in a learning way, by humbly asking the resolution of his doubts, acknowledging the weakness of his own understanding, and the superiority of his teachers. This is the common ruin of raw professors, that they presently grow proud of a poor ignorant head, as if it were full of knowledge and spirituality: and while they continue hearers, they continue not *disciples* or *learners*, but come with a proud and carping humour, to quarrel with their teachers, as poor ignorant men in comparison of them; and, therefore, choose them a heap of teachers according to their own opinions: and all this while they have such a desire to be somebody, and to vent their seeming wisdom, that they can hardly stay from being teachers themselves, till they have anything like a lawful call. Whereas, if they would have kept in the rank of humble learners till they had grown wiser, they might have preserved the church's peace and their own.

It is an easy thing to turn the native heat of religion into the feverish outside zeal about words, or circumstances, or ceremonies, whether it be for or against them. I know that one party will cry up *order*, and the other will cry up *spirituality*, and both will say that God maketh not light of the smallest matters in religion, nor must we: and in this general position there is some truth.

It would make a knowing Christian weep to see in these times what censures, and worse, are used on both sides about the wording of our prayers to God! How vile and unsufferable some account them that will pray in any words that are not *written down for them!* And how unlawful others account it to pray in their written forms: some because they are forms, and some because that Papists have used them, and some because they are, or have been, imposed! When God hath given them no command, but to pray in faith and fervency, according to the states of themselves and others, and in such order as is agreeable to the matter, and in such method as he hath given them a rule and pattern of. But of all quarrels about *forms* and *words*, he hath never made any of their particular determinations, no more than whether I shall study the words, or if necessity require it, preach extempore.

It is a wonder how they that believe the Scriptures, came first to make themselves believe that God maketh such a matter as they do, of their several words and forms of prayer: that he loveth only *extemporary* prayers, as some think, and hateth all prescribed forms; or that he loveth only prescribed forms, as others think, and hateth all extemporary prayers. Certainly in Christ's time both liturgies by *forms*, and also extemporary prayers, were used; and yet Christ never interposed in the controversy, so as to condemn the one or the other. He condemneth the Pharisees for making *long prayers* to cover their *devouring widows' houses*, and for their praying to be seen of men; but whether their prayers were a set form, or whether they were extemporary, he taketh no notice, as telling us that he condemned neither. (And it is likely the Pharisees' long form was, in many things, worse than ours, though the Psalms were a great part of it: and yet Christ and his apostles oft joined with them, and never condemned them.) Nay, as far as I can find, the Pharisees and other Jews were not in this so blind and quarrelsome as we; nor ever made a controversy of it, nor ever presumed to condemn either form or extemporary prayers.

Is it not by the law of nature the parents' duty to teach their children the Lord's Prayer, or a psalm, though it be a form? and why not then other words which are agreeable to their state? And He that taught his own disciples a form and rule of prayer, and telleth us that so "John taught his disciples," saith also to his apostles, "As my Father hath sent me, so send I you." The truth is, by making them teachers of his church, he did allow them to teach either by forms or without, as the case required. All the Scripture is now to preachers a form of teaching: and when we read a chapter, we read a prescribed form of doctrine; and it hath many forms of prayer and praise, and forms of baptizing, and administering the Lord's supper. If you say that the apostles had an infallible spirit, I answer, True: and that proveth that their doctrine was more infallible than other men's; but not that they only, and not other men, may teach by the way of forms: therefore let us learn to be more merciful and moderate in our judgment.

An affection of singularity in indifferent things doth either come from such ignorance as those were guilty of, (Rom. xiv,) or most commonly from pride, though you perceive it not yourselves.

If it be to go in a meaner garb than others, and, as some, not to put off the hat; or, as others, to go barefoot, or in a distinguishing habit; that all men may see, and say, This is a singular person in religion: it is easy to see how this gratifieth pride. Humility desireth not to be especially taken notice of; and in all things lawful to do as others do, doth gratify humility. It is strange to see how much stress some people lay upon their singular modes of worship, habits, gestures, and expressions, when they have taken them up! They would have all to follow them. Here you see the mystic Pharisee! Paul became a Jew to the Jews, and all things lawful to all men, to save some. 1 Cor. ix, 19, 20. I pray you mark his words. It had been no strange thing, if he had become wise to win the foolish, and showed himself strong to win the weak, &c.; but to become as a Jew when he circumcised Timothy, and shaved his head because he had a vow, and to be as under the law, to them that are under the law, without law to them that are without law, and to become as weak to them that are weak, to be made all things lawful to all men to save some— this is far from the religion of proud pretenders.

What abundance of things do many now blame and censure others for as temporizers, which they have nothing against, (that may be called reason,) but only that their neighbours use them? If a man stand up at the profession of the belief, or when psalms or hymns of praise to God are sung, he conformeth to the gestures of the congregation; this is made his dispraise, which is his praise. Is not standing a fit gesture to profess our faith in, and to praise God? Or is it praiseworthy to be odd and singular in the church, and not to do as the congregation doth? Austin professed his resolution, in all such gestures and lawful orders, to do as the church did where he was; and Paul would have us with one mouth, as well as with one mind, to glorify God. I entreat these men to mark whether it was Christ or the Pharisees that came nearest to their way, and whom they most imitate? Was it for going too far from sinners that the Pharisees censured Christ? or was it not for eating and drinking with them? though he did it not to harden them in their sin; but as a physician with the sick, to heal them. The case is plain; but corrupt nature more favoureth the separating zeal of the Pharisees than the loving, winning zeal of Christ, and makes it much easier to be imitators of them, than of him. This going too far from those we should win, doth not only lose our advantage, but greatly tendeth to harden them in all their prejudices against a religious life, and hinder their conversion, and so undo their souls.

In a word, woe be to the reformer who feareth not running to the extreme contrary to the error and sin which he would reform. Think and talk more of your faults and failings against others, than of theirs against you; and if you fall into the company of backbiters, that are dishonouring their rulers or their pastors, or who are telling how bad their neighbours are, labour to purify these stinking waters, or turn the stream: say to them, O friends, how bad are we ourselves! what pride is in our hearts! what ignorance in our minds! so wanting are we even in the lowest grace, humility, that we have scarce enough to make us take patiently such censures as we are now pouring out upon others. Take notice of all the good which appeareth in others. Be more in commendation of all the good which indeed is in them who differ from you in opinion. First, you would show yourselves more like to God, who is love, and unlike to Satan the accuser. Secondly, you would show an honest impartial ingenuity, which honoureth virtue wherever it is found. Thirdly, you would show an humble sense of your own frailty, who dare not proudly contemn your brethren. Fourthly, you would show more love to God himself, when you love all that is of God, wherever [sic] you discern it, and cannot bear to hear his gifts and mercies undervalued.

Remember also that you have never learned the Christian art of suffering aright, till you can suffer not only by bad men, but by men that otherwise are good; not only by enemies, but by friends; not only by them that bear the sword, but also by some who preach the word: and till you will not by oppression be made mad, nor driven from your innocency.

Even those forms of liturgy which now are most distasted, were brought in by the most zealous religious people at first. The many short invocations, versicles, and responses, which the people use, were brought in when the souls of the faithful did abound with zeal, and break out in holy fervors into such expressions, and could not well endure to be mere auditors, and not vocally bear their part in the praises of God, and prayers of the church. And in time those very words which signified their raptures, were used by formal hypocrites, without their zeal who first expressed them; and so being made dead images, and used by rote, in a senseless canting, it has now become a point of zeal to avoid them as unlawful, though they were received from the predecessors in piety of those men that now refuse them. But though the highest expressions of zeal are most loathsome when counterfeited, and turned into a mere lifeless form; yet it is the privation of life which is the fault of the thing, and not the thing in itself. Restore the same spirit to those words, and they will be as good as they were at the beginning. What is the inference from all this? Why, first, I would advise you to look more to the things themselves, and less to the persons; and regard the honour of humanity, if you regard not the honour of religion. Secondly, that you truly understand what interest such zealous persons as yourselves had in those opinions, forms, and practices, at the first; that if you will avoid them for some men's sake, you may think the better of them for other men's, so far as to bring you to some impartiality, and a pacific spirit. Thirdly, that you suspect that zeal in yourselves, which you think so much miscarried in your ancestors.

Of all parts of religion, (I know not how it comes to pass) men think that *negatives* are sufficient for *peace*. If a man live not unpeaceably, nor provoke any to wrath, he is thought a sufficient friend to peace; and therefore it is that love and peace do so little prosper. When Satan and his instruments do all that they can by fraud and force against it, we think it enough to stand by and do no harm. It is the *peacemakers* that Christ pronounceth *blessed*. Matt. v, 9. Here he that is not with Christ and the church is against it. Why should we think so much diligence in hearing, reading, praying, &c. is necessary to the promoting other parts of holiness, and nothing necessary to love and peace, but to do no hurt? Is it not *worthy* our labour? And is not our labour here as needful as anywhere? Judge by the multitude and quality of the adversaries, and by their power and success. It is a mark of hypocrisy to go no farther in our duties of godliness, than the safety of our reputation will give us leave. And is it not so in the duties of love and peace? If the kingdom of God be righteousness and peace, then what we would do to promote God's kingdom, we must do for them. Rom. xiv, 17. And if dividing Christ's kingdom is the way to destroy it, (and Satan is wiser than to divide his own kingdom, Matt. xii,) then whatever we would do to save the kingdom of Christ, all that we must do to preserve and restore the peace of it, and to heal its wounds.

Quest. But what would you have us do for love and peace, and against its contraries?

Answ. First, *preach* and *write* if it be your calling. Secondly, let the cause of love and peace be much in your open and secret prayers to God. Thirdly, instruct all that learn of you with principles of love and peace; and labour to plant them deep in their minds, and make them as sensible of the evil of the contraries, as of any other sin. Unless divines and parents do take this way of bringing up the people and children in this kind of doctrine, that love and peace may become their religion, the church is never likely to be recovered. Fourthly, in all your conference, labour (seasonably and prudently) to inculcate these matters on the hearers' minds, and to bear your testimony against cruelty and division. Fifthly, put such books into people's hands as plead best the cause of love and peace; among others, get men to read these:— Bishop Usher's Sermon on Eph. iv, 3; Bishop Hall's Peacemaker; Mr. Jeremiah Burroughs Heart Divisions; and Mr. Stillingfleet's Irenicum; and all Mr. Duries. Sixthly, disgrace not your doctrine by the badness of your lives; but be as much more holy than they are, as you are more peaceable, that they may see it is not a carnal unholy peace that you desire. But these things belong to the following directions: "Finally, brethren, farewell. Be perfect, be of good comfort, be of one mind, live in peace; and the God of love and peace shall be with you." 2 Cor. xiii, 11; Phil. iv, 9; 1 Thess. v, 23. "And the God of peace shall bruise Satan under your feet shortly." Rom. xvi, 20. "Now the God of peace be with you all. Amen." Rom. xv, 33.

Martyrdom for love and peace is as honourable and gainful, as martyrdom for the faith.

Directions to the Pastors Both to Prevent and Heal Divisions.

The practice of which, the author doth humbly and earnestly beg of them, as with tears, upon his knees, for the sake of Christ, that purchased the weakest with his blood; for the sake of those who hope to live in peace with Christ for ever; for the sake of those who are in danger of turning to errors, or contemning godliness, through the scandal of our divisions, to their damnation; for the sake of the church; for the sake of the rulers, that they may have the comfort of governing a quiet and united people; and for their own sakes, that they may give up their account with joy to the chief Shepherd and Bishop of our souls, and not with terror for the consuming and scattering of his flock. And the author humbly beggeth of them all, that this country may but *see* and *feel* that the pastors do understand, believe, consider, and obey, that will of God which these texts of Scripture do express: — Psa. xv, 4; Matthew xxv, 40, 45; xviii, 6, 10; 2 Cor. iv, 3; 1 Cor. ix, 16; Acts xx, 20, 24, 28, 33; 1 Pet. v, 2, 3; Luke xxii, 24, 25; 1 Thess. v, 12, 13; 1 Timothy v, 17; Phil. i, 15-18; Acts xxviii, 30, 31; Romans xiv, 1-4; xv, 1-7; xiv, 17-20.

Alas! our preaching, praying, conference, and living, tell all the world that we are weak. How few are there that be not either ignorant, or injudicious, or imprudent, or dull and lifeless, or dry and barren, or of a stammering tongue, in our ministerial work! And in so high a work, any one of these is a loathsome blemish. If we are put to defend our religion, or any necessary part thereof, how weakly and injudiciously is it usually done! In a word, our great divisions among ourselves, with our censures and usage of one another, do tell all the world not only that we are weak, but that too many of us account one another to be worse than weak, even intolerable. And shall we, by our weakness and faultiness, become the people's scandal, and tempt them to undue separations; and when we have done, be impatient with their weakness, while we overlook our own?

When the young and ungrounded sort of Christians do, by their errors, pride, or passions, disturb the church's peace and order, it is the pastors that are usually first assaulted by their abuses, and, therefore, are most impatient and exasperated against them. And it were well if we were so innocent ourselves, as that our consciences need not call us to inquire whether this be not partly the fruit of our own miscarriages. However, seeing both the eminency of our grace, and the nature of our office, should make us more sensible of the church's dangers, and more solicitous of its safety, than the private members are; I think that the chief part of the duty is incumbent upon us, which must be done in order for the prevention of these maladies and for the cure. And, therefore, I think that the principal work of a director in this case, must be with the ministers of Christ themselves. The church's peace lieth chiefly upon our hands; and if we miscarry, and will not understand instruction, nor bear admonition, nor do our parts, how little hope will be left of our tranquillity. The body must needs languish, when the physician is as bad as the disease.

On every side it is the pastors of the flocks that are accused, by those of the adverse party, as the chief offenders. One side saith, "It is you that teach the people errors, and put scruples into their minds, and lead them into contempt of order and authority;" and the other side saith, "It is you that proudly usurp authority which Christ never gave you, and lord it over God's heritage, and, by your own invention, lay snares before the people to divide them, and will not suffer them to unite in their proper centre, and agree in the primitive simplicity." And while each side is thus accused by the other, they have all the greater cause to suspect themselves; because it seemeth to be agreed on all hands, that it is the pastors who are principally in fault, though it be not agreed what the fault is, nor which party of the pastors must bear the blame.

And, indeed, where are there any factions but there are ministers that head them, and that both caused them at first, and keep them up? It is but reasonable, therefore, that we all suspect and search ourselves, and perhaps the lot may find out that Achan who is thought most innocent; and Jonah, who is not the worst in the ship, may be the man; and he may be the Judas who is last in asking, Master, is it I?

Besides all that shall be intimated in the following directions, these causes of the people's weakness and divisions are so openly manifest in too many pastors, that they cannot be concealed or excused.

First. There is so much ignorance in many, that they are not able judiciously to edify the flocks, nor to teach sound principles in a suitable manner and method to their hearers. Who can teach others that which they never learned themselves?

Secondly. Too many know not the weaknesses of the vulgar, and, therefore, neither justly resolve their doubts, nor answer their objections.

Thirdly. And how cold and unskilful are many in the application of that doctrine which they have tolerably opened; and speak the truths of the living God without any affecting reverence or gravity; and talk as drowsily of the evil of sin, the need of grace, the love of God in Jesus Christ, yea, of death and judgment, heaven and hell, as if it were their design to rock their hearers to sleep, or make them believe that it is but an historical fiction which they act, and that nothing they say is to be believed! There is no need of any more forcible means to entice men to sin, than to hear it preached against so coldly: nor is there need of any more to teach men to set light by Christ and grace, and heaven itself, than to hear them so heartlessly commended. We speak a few good words to the people in a reading tone, like a child that is saying his lesson, as if we believed not ourselves: and then we blame the people for being no more edified by us; and we look they should be much affected with that which never much affected the speakers. If Christ himself, who preached with authority, and used to awaken them with an *"He that hath ears to hear, let him hear,"* did yet convert no more than he did; what can we expect upon our drowsy and dry discourses, but drowsiness in the hearers, if not contempt?

The aforesaid unacquaintedness with the people and their weaknesses, doth make many teachers lose their labour, while they measure the common people by themselves. And, therefore, experience hath ofttimes constrained me to say, that, after all their learning in the universities, such pastors as never conversed familiarly with the poor and vulgar of the flock, and tried the exercise of personal instruction upon them, are no more to be regarded in any controversies about the pastoral work and discipline, than an unexperienced physician, or pilot, in many cases of their professions; which maketh many learned, self-conceited doctors, become the plagues, while they think themselves the pillars, of the church. Some make a formality and a snare of the gift of extemporary expression, and by a preposterous care to avoid all forms, teach not the people with that diligence which is necessary, but leave their minds void of those orderly, well-settled, secondary means, which should help the first; and thus, while some neglect the soul of religion, others neglect the body of it: between them both it is almost all too much neglected.

It is needful to the people's edification and union, that their pastors excel them much in knowledge and utterance, also in prudence, holiness, and heavenliness of mind and life. Because God useth to work by means, and vary the success according to the quality of the means and instruments, we may well conclude that the gifts and holiness of the pastors are very excellent and needful helps to the people's settled piety and peace. Where these are wanting, the order and means are wanting, by which God useth to convey his blessing.

Our grave attire will go but a little way to keep up our reputation, without some better testimony of our worth.

An empty head, a stammering tongue; dry, dull, and dis-orderly preaching; senseless, cold, or confused praying; vain and frothy conversation; will much abate the rever-ence of our persons.

It is their double measure of the spirit of wisdom and goodness, which must procure a double measure of honour to the ministry. If we excel ever so much in learning, it will not suffice, unless we excel in our proper ministerial gifts— preaching, exhortation, and prayer, which are the works of our office. Yea, though we excel them in all these abilities, it will not serve the ends of our ministry, unless we excel them in holiness, and every Christian virtue. The devil knoweth more than ministers; and if he have a tongue, he wanteth not utterance. He is the most excellent and honourable who is most like God, and hath most of his image. God hath more proposed himself to man's imitation in goodness, than in greatness: he hath not said, "Be great; for the Lord your God is great;" but, "Walk in the light, as he is in the light;" "Be ye holy; for the Lord your God is holy." To be great and bad, is to be able to do mischief: to be learned or ingenious and bad, is to be wise to do evil, and to be a crafty, subtle instrument, of the devil. Jeremiah iv, 22. It was no laud-able description of Elymas. Acts xiii, 8, 10. Satan never would transform himself into an angel of light, nor his ministers into the ministers of righteousness; nor would Pharisees and hypocrites cover oppression by long prayers; if light, righteousness, and long prayers, were not laudable in themselves, and necessary in the preachers of the word of God, and had not the ap-pearance of good in them, as a cloak for wickedness.

If therefore Satan, or any of his ministers, would have men credit their falsehood and wickedness, they must pretend to light and holiness. He that would keep up the true honour of his ministry, and be accepted with God, and esteemed by good men, must do it by real light and holiness. An ungodly minister hath a rooted enmity to the holy doctrine which he preacheth, and holy duties and life which he exhorteth the people to. How well, sincerely, readily, faithfully, they are like to do the work which they are enemies to, you may easily judge. Rom. viii, 7. I know that they are not enemies to the honour and maintenance, and therefore may force themselves to do much of the outside work; but where there is an inward enmity to the life and ends of it, we can expect but a formal, inconstant, discharge of such unpleasing duty. Truth is for goodness: the knowledge which maketh you not good is lost, and hath missed its end. If therefore your love to God and man, your mortification and unblameableness of life, your spiritual mindedness, be no greater than the people's, (or perhaps much less,) do not wonder if you lose your honour with them, and grow very contemptible in their eyes. Mal. i, 10, 14; ii; 1 Sam. ii, 17, 24, 30. If, as Moses, you stand nearer to God than the people do, you must be more holy than they; and your face must shine with the beams of God in the people's eyes.

If ever the church is healed of its wounds, it must be by the peaceable disposition of the pastors and people. If ever men come to a peaceable disposition, it must be by peaceable doctrine and principles; by a full and frequent explication of the nature, pre-eminence, and power of love; that they may hear of it so much, and so long, till love be made their religion, and become as the natural heat and constitution of their souls. To promote this, the aged, experienced, and ripe kind of ministers, and private kind of Christians, must instil it into young Christians and scholars, that they may have nothing so common in their ears and studies as uniting love.

If I knew that man by whom the salvation of my flock were like to be more promoted than by me, (whatever infirmity of my people might be the cause,)

I should think myself a servant of Satan, and an enemy of souls, if I were against it. So Christ be preached,
and the people instructed, sanctified, and saved; what
if it be done by another rather than by me? have I not
liberty to do my best? Shall I oppose the gospel and
its success? God forbid that I, or any faithful minister,
should be guilty of so odious a sin! I speak without
respect of persons. It is easy and common, both in
churches and private assemblies, to preach ourselves
while we seem to be preaching Christ; and by our perverse preaching to seek disciples for ourselves, even
when we are preaching up self-denial, and seem most
zealous for the saving of souls. Acts xx, 30.

He is the strongest Christian, and the most godly man,
who hath the greatest love to God, and heavenliness of
mind and life. And this may be the case of many a one,
who, by some error about the circumstances of discipline
and worship, is yet under some mistake. He that
offendeth me by his mistake, though he be weak in judgment in some points, may yet be a far stronger Christian
than I who see his error. He may have more love to God
and man; more humility and self-denial, &c. Let us therefore esteem men according to the image of God upon
them, and not despise them as weak in grace, because
they are weak in this point of knowledge: though still
their errors are not to be owned.

Beware of following the heated leaders of a party, and
of assuming the lead yourselves; for those who follow you,
when God showeth them mercy, they will repent, and
give you but little thanks for your labour. The disorders
of the church may convince us of our error in following
those whom we should have led into better discipline.

There are not many of the tumults that have cost the
lives of thousands about religion, but are kindled by the
young injudicious professors. Historians tell that when
King Francis, of France, had forbidden the reproaching

of the Popish way of worship, and silenced the ministers for not obeying him; many of the hot-brained people took this way of provoking him, by hanging up pictures and libels in the streets, (but that was not the way of God,) and began that persecution (by provoking the king) which cost many thousands, if not hundred thousands, their lives before it ended. And the *synod* at Rochel, which refused the grave counsel of Duplesses, Dumullen, and many others, were stirred up by the people's zeal, and ended in the blood of many score thousands, and the ruin of the power of the Protestants in France. Abundance of such sad instances might be given, if England needed to go anywhere else for matter of warning than to itself. He that after the experience of this age, will think it fit to follow the conduct of injudicious zealots, will be left as inexcusable as any man who never had a sight of hell.

But if you will do all things good and lawful to win men, and offend them by no unnecessary thing, and yet stand your ground, and stir not an inch from truth and soberness, piety or peace, to please any people in the world, this way shall do your work.

Let it also be observed, When pastors fall into parties, they always draw the people after them. Some take one side and some the other. If the officers divide, the soldiers will. If one side suppresses the other, it will nevertheless increase the schism, while the people will pity and plead for the party that is troden [sic] down. As to the younger and emptier sort of ministers, it is no wonder if they understand not that which they never had opportunity to study, or have taken but a taste of; but it were to be wished that they were so humble, as to confess that they are yet but beardless, and that time and long study is necessary to make them as wise as they think they are. O that the ministers of Christ were once sensible, not here only, but through all the Christian world, what a plague the conjunction of their ignorance, contentiousness, and their dividing, selfish zeal, hath been to the church of Christ! And what they have done against the souls of men, by violence and by heading parties, and by laying heaven and hell, and the salvation of their souls, upon the opinions which they never understood; by departing from the primitive simplicity, to maintain their side and sanctity by backbiting and reproaching others, whose persons perhaps they never saw, nor ever once soberly discoursed with face to face. Yet they make it their piety to revile by hearsay, and judge in a cause they never heard, nor understood. If ever God show mercy to his church, he will give them pastors after his own heart, who shall abound in light and love; and lead the people into concord upon the ancient terms; and make it their work to put this love-killing spirit to death, whether it work by striving disputes, or dividing principles and practices, or by reproaching others; by corporeal cruelty, or by a religious, censorious cruelty, which doth not kill nor strike men; but unchurch and damn them.

Are not the *sons* of Levi yet refined, when they have been in so many furnaces, and so long? When wisdom, holiness, and humility, are their nature, and selfish pride and worldliness are cured, this wrinkled, malignant enmity, will then cease, and an honest emulation to excel one another in wisdom, love, and all good works, will then take place; and then we shall not, like drunken men, one day fight and wound each other, and the next cry out of our wounds, and yet go on in our drunken fits to make them still wider.

I shall end these directions by recommending the following scriptures, which by the blessing of God may lead you to the spirit and practices I have been treating of: — Isa. ix, 6, 7; xl. 11; xlii, 1-4; xliv, 3-5; Ezek. xxxiv, 2-5; Isa. xi, lxv, xxv; ii, 3-5; Mal. ii, 5-10; Zec. ix, 9; Matt. xi, 29; Luke iv, 18; Mark iii, 21; John iv, 32, 34; ix, 4; Luke xxii, 24; Matt. xx, 25-27; John xviii, 36; Luke xii, 14; 1 Pet. v, 2-

4; 2 Cor. i, 24; Matt. xxiii, 8; 1 Cor. iv, 1-3; 2 Cor. x, 8; xiii, 10; Acts xiii, 18-20, 29-34; 2 Cor. xii, 5; 2 Tim. ii, 23-25; 1 Tim. iii, 2, 3; Tit. i, 7-10; 2 Cor. x, 3-5; Rom. xiv, 1; xv, 2, 3; Phil. iii, 15, 16; Eph. iv, 2, 3; Phil. ii, 3; James iii, 17; 1 Thess. ii, 5-7; Gal. v, 22; 2 Cor. x, 1; Gal. vi, 1; Col. iii, 12, 13; 1 Tim. vi, 11; Tit. iii, 2; 1 Pet. iii, 4; Lev. xix, 18; Rom. xii, 9, 10; xiii, 10; John xiii, 34, 35; xv, 12, 17; Gal. v, 14; 1 Thess. iv, 9; 1 Pet. i, 22; ii, 23; Matt. v, 44, 45; vi;14; v, 39-41; 1 Thess. v, 12-14; 1 Cor.ix,19.

Question. To what purpose do you set together all these words of Scripture, without any exposition, or telling us what you conclude from them?

Answer. I avoid all glosses, that you may not say, I have imposed anything of my own upon you, which is not the mind of your Lord himself. I set them together, that such as overlook them may have a deeper sense than they have had, first, of what is the true spirit of a Christian; secondly, of what is the office of the ministry, and which way they are to win souls, silence gainsayers, extirpate errors, prevent or cure schisms, and secure the church's peace.

As for those who can seriously read all these words of the Spirit of God, and yet can find in them no matter of correction, without a commentary and argumentations, I have no more to say to them at this time, but to add Christ's next words, John xiii, 18: "I speak not of you all: I know whom I have chosen." I shall annex a few texts that characterize a spirit contrary to Christianity, and the faithful ministry, and with them I shall conclude:— 1 John iii, 12, 13; Heb. xi, 4; John viii, 44; 1 Sam. xxv, 25; xxii; Ezra iv, 13, 15-17; Esther iii, 8; Dan. iii, 12; vi, 5; Amos vii, 12, 13; Matthew xxiii, 29-31; John xi, 48; Acts iv, 1, 2, 17, 18; Gal. iv, 29; 3 John 9-11; 1 Thess. ii, 14, 15; Luke ix, 54, 55.

THE END.

MEMBERS OF SCHMUL'S WESLEYAN BOOK CLUB
BUY THESE OUTSTANDING BOOKS AT 40% OFF
THE RETAIL PRICE

Join Schmul's Wesleyan Book Club by calling toll-free:
800-S$_7$P$_7$B$_2$O$_6$O$_6$K$_5$S$_7$

Put a discount Christian bookstore in your
own mailbox

Visit us on the Internet at
www.wesleyanbooks.com

Schmul Publishing Company | PO Box 776 | Nicholasville, KY 40340

Made in United States
Orlando, FL
21 March 2023